REVOLUTION

AND OTHER ESSAYS

Jack London

1st WORLD
LIBRARY
Literary Society

Revolution and Other Essays

Jack London

© 1st World Library, 2006
PO Box 2211
Fairfield, IA 52556
www.1stworldlibrary.com
First Edition

LCCN: 2006938069

Softcover ISBN: 978-1-4218-3362-0
Hardcover ISBN: 978-1-4218-3262-3
eBook ISBN: 978-1-4218-3462-7

Purchase *"Revolution and Other Essays"*
as a traditional bound book at:
www.1stWorldLibrary.com/purchase.asp?ISBN= 978-1-4218-3362-0

1st World Library is a literary, educational organization dedicated to:

- Creating a free internet library of downloadable ebooks

- Hosting writing competitions and offering book publishing scholarships.

Interested in more 1st World Library books?
contact: literacy@1stworldlibrary.com
Check us out at: www.1stworldlibrary.com

1st World Library Literary Society

Giving Back to the World

"If you want to work on the core problem, it's early school literacy."

- James Barksdale, former CEO of Netscape

"No skill is more crucial to the future of a child, or to a democratic and prosperous society, than literacy."

- Los Angeles Times

Literacy... means far more than learning how to read and write... The aim is to transmit... knowledge and promote social participation."

- UNESCO

"Literacy is not a luxury, it is a right and a responsibility. If our world is to meet the challenges of the twenty-first century we must harness the energy and creativity of all our citizens."

- President Bill Clinton

"Parents should be encouraged to read to their children, and teachers should be equipped with all available techniques for teaching literacy, so the varying needs and capacities of individual kids can be taken into account."

- Hugh Mackay

CONTENTS

REVOLUTION

"The present is enough for common souls,
Who, never looking forward, are indeed
Mere clay, wherein the footprints of their age
Are petrified for ever."

I received a letter the other day. It was from a man in Arizona. It began, "Dear Comrade." It ended, "Yours for the Revolution." I replied to the letter, and my letter began, "Dear Comrade." It ended, "Yours for the Revolution." In the United States there are 400,000 men, of men and women nearly 1,000,000, who begin their letters "Dear Comrade," and end them "Yours for the Revolution." In Germany there are 3,000,000 men who begin their letters "Dear Comrade" and end them "Yours for the Revolution"; in France, 1,000,000 men; in Austria, 800,000 men; in Belgium, 300,000 men; in Italy, 250,000 men; in England, 100,000 men; in Switzerland, 100,000 men; in Denmark, 55,000 men; in Sweden, 50,000 men; in Holland, 40,000 men; in Spain, 30,000 men—comrades all, and revolutionists.

These are numbers which dwarf the grand armies of Napoleon and Xerxes. But they are numbers not of conquest and maintenance of the established order, but of conquest and revolution. They compose, when the roll is called, an army of 7,000,000 men, who, in accordance with the conditions of to-day, are fighting with all their might for the conquest of the wealth of the world and for the complete overthrow of existing society.

There has never been anything like this revolution in the history of the world. There is nothing analogous between it and the American Revolution or the French Revolution. It is unique, colossal. Other revolutions compare with it as asteroids compare with the sun. It is alone of its kind, the first world-revolution in a world whose history is replete with revolutions. And not only this, for it is the first organized movement of men to become a world movement, limited only by the limits of the planet.

This revolution is unlike all other revolutions in many respects. It is not sporadic. It is not a flame of popular discontent, arising in a day and dying down in a day. It is older than the present generation. It has a history and traditions, and a martyr-roll only less extensive possibly than the martyr-roll of Christianity. It has also a literature a myriad times more imposing, scientific, and scholarly than the literature of any previous revolution.

They call themselves "comrades," these men, comrades in the socialist revolution. Nor is the word empty and meaningless, coined of mere lip service. It knits men together as brothers, as men should be knit together who stand shoulder to shoulder under the red banner of revolt. This red banner, by the way, symbolizes the brotherhood of man, and does not symbolize the incendiarism that instantly connects itself with the red banner in the affrighted bourgeois mind. The comradeship of the revolutionists is alive and warm. It passes over geographical lines, transcends race prejudice, and has even proved itself mightier than the Fourth of July, spread-eagle Americanism of our forefathers. The French socialist working-men and the German socialist working-men forget Alsace and Lorraine, and, when war threatens, pass resolutions declaring that as working-men and comrades they have no quarrel with each other. Only the other day, when Japan and Russia sprang at each other's throats, the revolutionists of Japan addressed the following message to the revolutionists of Russia: "Dear

Comrades—Your government and ours have recently plunged into war to carry out their imperialistic tendencies, but for us socialists there are no boundaries, race, country, or nationality. We are comrades, brothers, and sisters, and have no reason to fight. Your enemies are not the Japanese people, but our militarism and so-called patriotism. Patriotism and militarism are our mutual enemies."

In January 1905, throughout the United States the socialists held mass-meetings to express their sympathy for their struggling comrades, the revolutionists of Russia, and, more to the point, to furnish the sinews of war by collecting money and cabling it to the Russian leaders. The fact of this call for money, and the ready response, and the very wording of the call, make a striking and practical demonstration of the international solidarity of this world-revolution:

"Whatever may be the immediate results of the present revolt in Russia, the socialist propaganda in that country has received from it an impetus unparalleled in the history of modern class wars. The heroic battle for freedom is being fought almost exclusively by the Russian working-class under the intellectual leadership of Russian socialists, thus once more demonstrating the fact that the class-conscious working-men have become the vanguard of all liberating movements of modern times."

Here are 7,000,000 comrades in an organized, international, world-wide, revolutionary movement. Here is a tremendous human force. It must be reckoned with. Here is power. And here is romance—romance so colossal that it seems to be beyond the ken of ordinary mortals. These revolutionists are swayed by great passion. They have a keen sense of personal right, much of reverence for humanity, but little reverence, if any at all, for the rule of the dead. They refuse to be ruled by the dead. To the bourgeois mind their unbelief in the dominant conventions of the established order is startling. They laugh to scorn the sweet ideals and dear moralities of bourgeois society. They intend to destroy bourgeois society with most of its sweet ideals and dear moralities, and chiefest among these are those that group themselves under such heads as private ownership of capital, survival of the fittest, and patriotism—even patriotism.

Such an army of revolution, 7,000,000 strong, is a thing to make rulers and ruling classes pause and consider. The cry of this army is, "No quarter! We want all that you possess. We will be content with nothing less than all that you possess. We want in our hands the reins of power and the destiny of mankind. Here are our hands. They are strong hands. We are going to take your governments, your palaces, and all your purpled ease away from you, and in that day you shall work for your bread even as the peasant in the field or the starved and runty clerk in your metropolises. Here are our hands. They are strong hands."

Well may rulers and ruling classes pause and consider. This is revolution. And, further, these 7,000,000 men are not an army on paper. Their fighting strength in the field is 7,000,000. To-day they cast 7,000,000 votes in the civilized countries of the world.

Yesterday they were not so strong. Tomorrow they will be still stronger. And they are fighters. They love peace. They are unafraid of war. They intend nothing less than to destroy existing capitalist society and to take possession of the whole world. If the law of the land permits, they fight for this end peaceably, at the ballot-box. If the law of the land does not permit, and if they have force meted out to them, they resort to force themselves. They meet violence with violence. Their hands are strong and they are unafraid. In Russia, for instance, there is no suffrage. The government executes the revolutionists. The revolutionists kill the officers of the government. The revolutionists meet legal murder with assassination.

Now here arises a particularly significant phase which it would be well for the rulers to consider. Let me make it concrete. I am a revolutionist. Yet I am a fairly sane and normal individual. I speak, and I THINK, of these assassins in Russia as "my comrades." So do all the comrades in America, and all the 7,000,000 comrades in the world. Of what worth an organized, international, revolutionary movement if our comrades are not backed up the world over! The worth is shown by the fact that we do back up the assassinations by our comrades in Russia. They are not disciples of Tolstoy, nor are we. We are revolutionists.

Our comrades in Russia have formed what they call "The Fighting Organization." This Fighting Organization accused, tried, found guilty, and condemned to death, one Sipiaguin, Minister of Interior. On April 2 he was shot and killed in the Maryinsky Palace. Two years later the Fighting Organization condemned to death and executed another Minister of Interior, Von Plehve. Having done so, it issued a document, dated July 29, 1904, setting forth the counts of its indictment of Von Plehve and its responsibility for the assassination. Now, and to the point, this document was sent out to the socialists of the world, and by them was published everywhere in the magazines and newspapers. The point is, not that the socialists of the world were unafraid to do it, not that they dared to do it, but that they did it as a matter of routine, giving publication to what may be called an official document of the international revolutionary movement.

These are high lights upon the revolution—granted, but they are also facts. And they are given to the rulers and the ruling classes, not in bravado, not to frighten them, but for them to consider more deeply the spirit and nature of this world-revolution. The time has come for the revolution to demand consideration. It has fastened upon every civilized country in the world. As fast as a country becomes civilized, the revolution fastens upon it. With the introduction of the machine into Japan, socialism was introduced. Socialism marched into the Philippines shoulder to shoulder with the American soldiers. The echoes of the last gun had scarcely died away when socialist locals were forming in Cuba and Porto Rico. Vastly more significant is the fact that of all the countries the revolution has fastened upon, on not one has it relaxed its grip. On the contrary, on every country its grip closes tighter year by year. As an active movement it began obscurely over a generation ago. In 1867, its voting strength in the world was 30,000. By 1871 its vote had increased to 1,000,000. Not till 1884 did it pass the half-million point. By 1889 it had passed the million point, it had then gained momentum. In 1892 the socialist vote of the world was 1,798,391; in 1893, 2,585,898; in 1895, 3,033,718; in 1898, 4,515,591; in 1902, 5,253,054; in 1903, 6,285,374; and in the year of our Lord 1905 it passed the seven-million mark.

Nor has this flame of revolution left the United States untouched. In 1888 there were only 2,068 socialist votes. In 1902 there were 127,713 socialist votes. And in 1904 435,040 socialist votes were cast. What fanned this flame? Not hard times. The first four years of the twentieth century were considered prosperous years, yet in that time more than 300,000 men added themselves to the ranks of the revolutionists, flinging their defiance in the teeth of bourgeois society and taking their stand under the blood-red banner. In the state of the writer, California, one man in twelve is an avowed and registered revolutionist.

One thing must be clearly understood. This is no spontaneous and vague uprising of a large mass of discontented and miserable people—a blind and instinctive recoil from hurt. On the contrary, the propaganda is intellectual; the movement is based upon economic necessity and is in line with social evolution; while the miserable people have not yet revolted. The revolutionist is no starved and diseased slave in the shambles at the bottom of the social pit, but is, in the main, a hearty, well-fed working-man, who sees the shambles waiting for him and his children and recoils from the descent. The very miserable people are too helpless to help themselves. But they are being helped, and the day is not far distant when their numbers will go to swell the ranks of the revolutionists.

Another thing must be clearly understood. In spite of the fact that middle-class men and professional men are interested in the movement, it is nevertheless a distinctly working-class revolt. The world over, it is a working-class revolt. The workers of the world, as a class, are fighting the capitalists of the world, as a class. The so-called great middle class is a growing anomaly in the social struggle. It is a perishing class (wily statisticians to the contrary), and its historic mission of buffer between the capitalist and working-classes has just about been fulfilled. Little remains for it but to wail as it passes into oblivion, as it has already begun to wail in accents Populistic and Jeffersonian-Democratic. The fight is on. The revolution is here now, and it is the world's workers that are in revolt.

Naturally the question arises: Why is this so? No mere whim of the spirit can give rise to a world-revolution. Whim does not conduce to unanimity. There must be a deep-seated cause to make 7,000,000 men of the one mind, to make them cast off allegiance to the bourgeois gods and lose faith in so fine a thing as patriotism. There are many counts of the indictment which the revolutionists bring against the capitalist class, but for present use only one need be stated, and it is a count to which capital has never replied and can never reply.

The capitalist class has managed society, and its management has failed. And not only has it failed in its management, but it has failed deplorably, ignobly, horribly. The capitalist class had an opportunity such as was vouchsafed no previous ruling class in the history of the world. It broke away from the rule of the old feudal aristocracy and made modern society. It mastered matter, organized the machinery of life, and made possible a wonderful era for mankind, wherein no creature should cry aloud because it had not enough to eat, and wherein for every child there would be opportunity for education, for intellectual and spiritual uplift. Matter being mastered, and the machinery of life organized, all this was possible. Here was the chance, God-given, and the capitalist class failed. It was blind and greedy. It prattled sweet ideals and dear moralities, rubbed its eyes not once, nor ceased one whit in its greediness, and smashed down in a failure as tremendous only as was the opportunity it had ignored.

But all this is like so much cobwebs to the bourgeois mind. As it was blind in the past, it is blind now and cannot see nor understand. Well, then, let the indictment be stated more definitely, in terms sharp and unmistakable. In the first place, consider the caveman. He was a very simple creature. His head slanted back like an orang-outang's, and he had but little more intelligence. He lived in a hostile environment, the prey of all manner of fierce life. He had no inventions nor artifices. His natural efficiency for food-getting was, say, 1. He did not even till the soil. With his natural efficiency of 1, he fought off his carnivorous enemies and got himself food and shelter. He must have done all this, else he would not have multiplied and spread over the earth and sent his progeny down, generation by generation, to become even you and me.

The caveman, with his natural efficiency of 1, got enough to eat most of the time, and no caveman went hungry all the time. Also, he lived a healthy, open-air life, loafed and rested himself, and found plenty of time in which to exercise his imagination and invent gods. That is to say, he did not have to work all his waking moments in order to get enough to eat. The child of the caveman (and this is true of the children of all savage peoples) had a childhood, and by that is meant a happy childhood of play and development.

And now, how fares modern man? Consider the United States, the most prosperous and most enlightened country of the world. In the United States there are 10,000,000 people living in poverty. By poverty is meant that condition in life in which, through lack of food and adequate shelter, the mere standard of working efficiency cannot be maintained. In the United States there are 10,000,000 people who have not enough to eat. In the United States, because they have not enough to eat, there are 10,000,000 people who cannot keep the ordinary 1 measure of strength in their bodies. This means that these 10,000,000 people are perishing, are dying, body and soul, slowly, because they have not enough to eat. All over this broad, prosperous, enlightened land, are men, women, and children who are living miserably. In all the great cities, where they are segregated in slum ghettos by hundreds of thousands and by millions, their misery becomes beastliness. No caveman ever starved as chronically as they starve, ever slept as vilely as they sleep, ever festered with rottenness and disease as they fester, nor ever toiled as hard and for as long hours as they toil.

In Chicago there is a woman who toiled sixty hours per week. She was a garment worker. She sewed buttons on clothes. Among the Italian garment workers of Chicago, the average weekly wage of the dressmakers is 90 cents, but they work every week in the year. The average weekly wage of the pants finishers is $1.31, and the average number of weeks employed in the year is 27.85. The average yearly earnings of the dressmakers is $37; of the pants finishers, $42.4l. Such wages means no childhood for the children, beastliness of living, and starvation for all.

Unlike the caveman, modern man cannot get food and shelter whenever he feels like working for it. Modern man has first to find the work, and in this he is often unsuccessful. Then misery becomes acute. This acute misery is chronicled daily in the newspapers. Let several of the countless instances be cited.

In New York City lived a woman, Mary Mead. She had three children: Mary, one year old; Johanna, two years old; Alice, four years old. Her husband could find no work. They starved. They were evicted from their shelter at 160 Steuben Street. Mary Mead strangled her baby, Mary, one year old; strangled Alice, four years old; failed to strangle Johanna, two years old, and then herself took poison. Said the father to the police: "Constant poverty had driven my wife insane. We lived at No. 160 Steuben Street until a week ago, when we were dispossessed. I could get no work. I could not even make enough to put food into our mouths. The babies grew ill and weak. My wife cried nearly all the time."

"So overwhelmed is the Department of Charities with tens of thousands of applications from men out of work that it finds itself unable to cope with the situation."—New York

Commercial, January 11, 1905.

In a daily paper, because he cannot get work in order to get something to eat, modern man advertises as follows:

"Young man, good education, unable to obtain employment, will sell to physician and bacteriologist for experimental purposes all right and title to his body. Address for price, box 3466, Examiner."

"Frank A. Mallin went to the central police station Wednesday night and asked to be locked up on a charge of vagrancy. He said he had been conducting an unsuccessful search for work for so long that he was sure he must be a vagrant. In any event, he was so hungry he must be fed. Police Judge Graham sentenced him to ninety days' imprisonment."—San Francisco Examiner.

In a room at the Soto House, 32 Fourth Street, San Francisco, was found the body of W. G. Robbins. He had turned on the gas. Also was found his diary, from which the following extracts are made

"March 3.—No chance of getting anything here. What will I do?

"March 7.—Cannot find anything yet.

"March 8.—Am living on doughnuts at five cents a day.

"March 9.—My last quarter gone for room rent.

"March 10.—God help me. Have only five cents left. Can get nothing to do. What next? Starvation or—? I have spent my last nickel to-night. What shall I do? Shall it be steal, beg, or die? I have never stolen, begged, or starved in all my fifty years of life, but now I am on the brink—death seems the only refuge.

"March 11.—Sick all day—burning fever this afternoon. Had nothing to eat to-day or since yesterday noon. My head, my head. Good-bye, all."

How fares the child of modern man in this most prosperous of lands? In the city of New York 50,000 children go hungry to school every morning. From the same city on January 12, a press despatch was sent out over the country of a case reported by Dr. A. E. Daniel, of the New York Infirmary for Women and Children. The case was that of a babe, eighteen months old, who earned by its labour fifty cents per week in a tenement sweat-shop.

"On a pile of rags in a room bare of furniture and freezing cold, Mrs. Mary Gallin, dead from starvation, with an emaciated baby four months old crying at her breast, was found this morning at 513 Myrtle Avenue, Brooklyn, by Policeman McConnon of the Flushing Avenue Station. Huddled together for warmth in another part of the room were the father, James Gallin, and three children ranging from two to eight years of age. The children gazed at the policeman much as ravenous animals might have done. They were famished, and there was not a vestige of food in their comfortless home."—New York Journal, January 2, 1902.

In the United States 80,000 children are toiling out their lives in the textile mills alone. In the South they work twelve-hour shifts. They never see the day. Those on the night shift are asleep when the sun pours its life and warmth over the world, while those on the day shift are at the machines before dawn and return to their miserable dens, called "homes," after dark. Many receive no more than ten cents a day. There are babies who work for five and six cents a day. Those who work on the night shift are often kept awake by having cold water dashed in their faces. There are children six years of age who have already to their credit eleven months' work on the night shift. When they become sick, and are unable to rise from their beds to go to work, there are men employed to go on horseback from house to house, and cajole and bully them into arising and going to work. Ten per cent of them contract active consumption. All are puny wrecks, distorted, stunted, mind and body. Elbert Hubbard says of the child-labourers of the Southern cotton-mills:

"I thought to lift one of the little toilers to ascertain his weight. Straightaway through his thirty-five pounds of skin and bones there ran a tremor of fear, and he struggled forward to tie a broken thread. I attracted his attention by a touch, and offered him a silver dime. He looked at me dumbly from a face that might have belonged to a man of sixty, so furrowed, tightly drawn, and full of pain it was. He did not reach for the money—he did not know what it was. There were dozens of such children in this particular mill. A physician who was with me said that they would all be dead probably in two years, and their places filled by others—there were plenty more. Pneumonia carries off most of them. Their systems are ripe for disease, and when it comes there is no rebound—no response. Medicine simply does not act—nature is whipped, beaten, discouraged, and the child sinks into a stupor and dies."

So fares modern man and the child of modern man in the United States, most prosperous and enlightened of all countries on earth. It must be remembered that the instances given are instances only, but they can be multiplied myriads of times. It must also be remembered that what is true of the United States is true of all the civilized world. Such misery was not true of the caveman. Then what has happened? Has the hostile environment of the caveman grown more hostile for his descendants? Has the caveman's natural efficiency of 1 for food-getting and shelter-getting diminished in modern man to one-half or one-quarter?

On the contrary, the hostile environment of the caveman has been destroyed. For modern man it no longer exists. All carnivorous enemies, the daily menace of the younger world, have been killed off. Many of the species of prey have become extinct. Here and there, in secluded portions of the world, still linger a few of man's fiercer enemies. But they are far from being a menace to mankind. Modern man, when he wants recreation and change, goes to the secluded portions of the world for a hunt. Also, in idle moments, he wails regretfully at the passing of the "big game," which he knows in the not distant future will disappear from the earth.

Nor since the day of the caveman has man's efficiency for food-getting and shelter-getting diminished. It has increased a thousandfold. Since the day of the caveman, matter has been mastered. The secrets of matter have been discovered. Its laws have been formulated. Wonderful artifices have been made, and marvellous inventions, all tending to increase tremendously man's natural efficiency of in every food-getting, shelter-getting exertion, in farming, mining, manufacturing, transportation, and communication.

From the caveman to the hand-workers of three generations ago, the increase in efficiency for food- and shelter-getting has been very great. But in this day, by machinery, the efficiency of the hand-worker of three generations ago has in turn been increased many times. Formerly it required 200 hours of human labour to place 100 tons of ore on a railroad car. To-day, aided by machinery, but two hours of human labour is required to do the same task. The United States Bureau of Labour is responsible for the following table, showing the comparatively recent increase in man's food- and shelter-getting efficiency:

	Machine Hours	Hand Hours
Barley (100 bushels)	9	211
Corn (50 bushels shelled, stalks, husks and blades cut into fodder)	34	228
Oats (160 bushels)	28	265
Wheat (50 bushels)	7	160

Loading ore (loading 100 tons iron ore on cars)	2	200
Unloading coal (transferring 200 tons from canal-boats to bins 400 feet distant)	20	240
Pitchforks (50 pitchforks, 12-inch tines)	12	200
Plough (one landside plough, oak beams and handles)	3	118

According to the same authority, under the best conditions for organization in farming, labour can produce 20 bushels of wheat for 66 cents, or 1 bushel for 3.5 cents. This was done on a bonanza farm of 10,000 acres in California, and was the average cost of the whole product of the farm. Mr. Carroll D. Wright says that to-day 4,500,000 men, aided by machinery, turn out a product that would require the labour of 40,000,000 men if produced by hand. Professor Herzog, of Austria, says that 5,000,000 people with the machinery of to-day, employed at socially useful labour, would be able to supply a population of 20,000,000 people with all the necessaries and small luxuries of life by working 1.5 hours per day.

This being so, matter being mastered, man's efficiency for food-and shelter-getting being increased a thousandfold over the efficiency of the caveman, then why is it that millions of modern men live more miserably than lived the caveman? This is the question the revolutionist asks, and he asks it of the managing class, the capitalist class. The capitalist class does not answer it. The capitalist class cannot answer it.

If modern man's food-and shelter-getting efficiency is a thousandfold greater than that of the caveman, why, then, are there 10,000,000 people in the United States to-day who are not properly sheltered and properly fed? If the child of the caveman did not have to work, why, then, to-day, in the United States, are 80,000 children working out their lives in the textile factories alone? If the child of the caveman did not have to work, why, then, to-day, in the United States, are there 1,752,187 child-labourers?

It is a true count in the indictment. The capitalist class has mismanaged, is to-day mismanaging. In New York City 50,000 children go hungry to school, and in New York City there are 1,320 millionaires. The point, however, is not that the mass of mankind is miserable because of the wealth the capitalist class has taken to itself. Far from it. The point really is that the mass of mankind is miserable, not for want of the wealth taken by the capitalist class, BUT FOR WANT OF THE WEALTH THAT WAS NEVER CREATED. This wealth was never created because the capitalist class managed too wastefully and irrationally. The capitalist class, blind and greedy, grasping madly, has not only not made the best of its management, but made the worst of it. It is a management prodigiously wasteful. This point cannot be emphasized too strongly.

In face of the facts that modern man lives more wretchedly than the caveman, and that modern man's food-and shelter-getting efficiency is a thousandfold greater than the caveman's, no other solution is possible than that the management is prodigiously wasteful.

With the natural resources of the world, the machinery already invented, a rational organization of production and distribution, and an equally rational elimination of waste, the able-bodied workers would not have to labour more than two or three hours per day to feed everybody, clothe everybody, house everybody, educate everybody, and give a fair measure of little luxuries to everybody. There would be no more material want and wretchedness, no more children toiling out their lives, no more men and women and babes living like beasts and dying like beasts. Not only would matter be mastered, but the machine would be mastered. In such a day incentive would be finer and nobler than the incentive of to-day, which is the incentive of the stomach. No man, woman, or child, would be impelled to action by an empty stomach. On the contrary, they would be impelled to action as a child in a spelling match is impelled to action, as boys and girls at games, as scientists formulating law, as inventors applying law, as artists and sculptors painting canvases and shaping clay, as poets and statesmen serving humanity by singing and by statecraft. The spiritual, intellectual, and artistic uplift consequent upon such a condition of society would be tremendous. All the human world would surge upward in a mighty wave.

This was the opportunity vouchsafed the capitalist class. Less blindness on its part, less greediness, and a rational management, were all that was necessary. A wonderful era was possible for the human race. But the capitalist class failed. It made a shambles of civilization. Nor can the capitalist class plead not guilty. It knew of the opportunity. Its wise men told of the opportunity, its scholars and its scientists told it of the opportunity. All that they said is there to-day in the books, just so much damning evidence against it. It would not listen. It was too greedy. It rose up (as it rises up to-day), shamelessly, in our legislative halls, and declared that profits were impossible without the toil of children and babes. It lulled its conscience to sleep with prattle of sweet ideals and dear moralities, and allowed the suffering and misery of mankind to continue and to increase, in short, the capitalist class failed to take advantage of the opportunity.

But the opportunity is still here. The capitalist class has been tried and found wanting. Remains the working-class to see what it can do with the opportunity. "But the working-class is incapable," says the capitalist class. "What do you know about it?" the working-class replies. "Because you have failed is no reason that we shall fail. Furthermore, we are going to have a try at it, anyway. Seven millions of us say so. And what have you to say to that?"

And what can the capitalist class say? Grant the incapacity of the working-class. Grant that the indictment and the argument of the revolutionists are all wrong. The 7,000,000 revolutionists remain. Their existence is a fact. Their belief in their capacity, and in their indictment and their argument, is a fact. Their constant growth is a fact. Their intention to destroy present-day society is a fact, as is also their intention to take possession of the world with all its wealth and machinery and governments. Moreover, it is a fact that the working-class is vastly larger than the capitalist class.

The revolution is a revolution of the working-class. How can the capitalist class, in the minority, stem this tide of revolution? What has it to offer? What does it offer? Employers' associations, injunctions, civil suits for plundering of the treasuries of the labour-unions, clamour and combination for the open shop, bitter and shameless opposition to the eight-hour day, strong efforts to defeat all reform, child-labour bills, graft in every municipal council, strong lobbies and bribery in every legislature for the purchase of capitalist legislation, bayonets, machine-guns, policemen's clubs, professional strike-breakers and armed Pinkertons—these are the things the capitalist class is dumping in front of the tide of revolution, as though, forsooth, to hold it back.

The capitalist class is as blind to-day to the menace of the revolution as it was blind in the past to its own God-given opportunity. It cannot see how precarious is its position, cannot comprehend the power and the portent of the revolution. It goes on its placid way, prattling sweet ideals and dear moralities, and scrambling sordidly for material benefits.

No overthrown ruler or class in the past ever considered the revolution that overthrew it, and so with the capitalist class of to-day. Instead of compromising, instead of lengthening its lease of life by conciliation and by removal of some of the harsher oppressions of the working-class, it antagonizes the working-class, drives the working-class into revolution. Every broken strike in recent years, every legally plundered trades-union treasury, every closed shop made into an open shop, has driven the members of the working-class directly hurt over to socialism by hundreds and thousands. Show a working-man that his union fails, and he becomes a revolutionist. Break a strike with an injunction or bankrupt a union with a civil suit, and the working-men hurt thereby listen to the siren song of the socialist and are lost for ever to the POLITICAL CAPITALIST parties.

Antagonism never lulled revolution, and antagonism is about all the capitalist class offers. It is true, it offers some few antiquated notions which were very efficacious in the past, but which are no longer efficacious. Fourth-of-July liberty in terms of the Declaration of Independence and of the French Encyclopaedists is scarcely apposite to-day. It does not appeal to the working-man who has had his head broken by a policeman's club, his union treasury bankrupted by a court decision, or his job taken away from him by a labour-saving invention. Nor does the Constitution of the United States appear so glorious and constitutional to the working-man who has experienced a bull-pen or been unconstitutionally deported from Colorado. Nor are this particular working-man's hurt feelings soothed by reading in the newspapers that both the bull-pen and the deportation were pre-eminently just, legal, and constitutional. "To hell, then, with the Constitution!" says he, and another revolutionist has been made—by the capitalist class.

In short, so blind is the capitalist class that it does nothing to lengthen its lease of life, while it does everything to shorten it. The capitalist class offers nothing that is clean, noble, and alive. The revolutionists offer everything that is clean, noble, and alive. They offer service, unselfishness, sacrifice, martyrdom—the things that sting awake the imagination of the people, touching their hearts with the fervour that arises out of the impulse toward good and which is essentially religious in its nature.

But the revolutionists blow hot and blow cold. They offer facts and statistics, economics and scientific arguments. If the working-man be merely selfish, the revolutionists show him, mathematically demonstrate to him, that his condition will be bettered by the revolution. If the working-man be the higher type, moved by impulses toward right conduct, if he have soul and spirit, the revolutionists offer him the things of the soul and the spirit, the tremendous things that cannot be measured by dollars and cents, nor be held down by dollars and cents. The revolutionist cries out upon wrong and injustice, and preaches righteousness. And, most potent of all, he sings the eternal song of human freedom—a song of all lands and all tongues and all time.

Few members of the capitalist class see the revolution. Most of them are too ignorant, and many are too afraid to see it. It is the same old story of every perishing ruling class in the world's history. Fat with power and possession, drunken with success, and made soft by surfeit and by cessation of struggle, they are like the drones clustered about the honey vats when the worker-bees spring upon them to end their rotund existence.

President Roosevelt vaguely sees the revolution, is frightened by it, and recoils from seeing it. As he says: "Above all, we need to remember that any kind of class animosity in the political world is, if possible, even more wicked, even more destructive to national welfare, than sectional, race, or religious animosity."

Class animosity in the political world, President Roosevelt maintains, is wicked. But class animosity in the political world is the preachment of the revolutionists. "Let the class wars in the industrial world continue," they say, "but extend the class war to the political world." As their leader, Eugene V. Debs says: "So far as this struggle is concerned, there is no good capitalist and no bad working-man. Every capitalist is your enemy and every working-man is your friend."

Here is class animosity in the political world with a vengeance. And here is revolution. In 1888 there were only 2,000 revolutionists of this type in the United States; in 1900 there were 127,000 revolutionists; in 1904, 435,000 revolutionists. Wickedness of the President Roosevelt definition evidently flourishes and increases in the United States. Quite so, for it is the revolution that flourishes and increases.

Here and there a member of the capitalist class catches a clear glimpse of the revolution, and raises a warning cry. But his class does not heed. President Eliot of Harvard raised such a cry:

"I am forced to believe there is a present danger of socialism never before so imminent in America in so dangerous a form, because never before imminent in so well organized a form. The danger lies in the obtaining control of the trades-unions by the socialists." And the capitalist employers, instead of giving heed to the warnings, are perfecting their strike-breaking organization and combining more strongly than ever for a general assault upon that dearest of all things to the trades-unions—the closed shop. In so far as this assault succeeds, by just that much will the capitalist class shorten its lease of life. It is the old, old story, over again and over again. The drunken drones still cluster greedily about the honey vats.

Possibly one of the most amusing spectacles of to-day is the attitude of the American press toward the revolution. It is also a pathetic spectacle. It compels the onlooker to be aware of a distinct loss of pride in his species. Dogmatic utterance from the mouth of ignorance may make gods laugh, but it should make men weep. And the American editors (in the general instance) are so impressive about it! The old "divide-up," "men-are-NOT-born-free-and-equal," propositions are enunciated gravely and sagely, as things white-hot and new from the forge of human wisdom. Their feeble vapourings show no more than a schoolboy's comprehension of the nature of the revolution. Parasites themselves on the capitalist class, serving the capitalist class by moulding public opinion, they, too, cluster drunkenly about the honey vats.

Of course, this is true only of the large majority of American editors. To say that it is true of all of them would be to cast too great obloquy upon the human race. Also, it would be untrue, for here and there an occasional editor does see clearly—and in his case, ruled by stomach-incentive, is usually afraid to say what he thinks about it. So far as the science and the sociology of the revolution are concerned, the average editor is a generation or so behind the facts. He is intellectually slothful, accepts no facts until they are accepted by the majority, and prides himself upon his conservatism. He is an instinctive optimist, prone to believe that what ought to be, is. The revolutionist gave this up long ago, and believes not that what ought to be, is, but what is, is, and that it may not be what it ought to be at all.

Now and then, rubbing his eyes, vigorously, an editor catches a sudden glimpse of the revolution and breaks out in naive volubility, as, for instance, the one who wrote the following in the Chicago Chronicle: "American socialists are revolutionists. They know that they are revolutionists. It is high time that other people should appreciate the fact." A white-hot, brand-new discovery, and he proceeded to shout it out from the housetops that we, forsooth, were revolutionists. Why, it is just what we have been doing all these years—shouting it out from the housetops that we are revolutionists, and stop us who can.

The time should be past for the mental attitude: "Revolution is atrocious. Sir, there is no revolution." Likewise should the time be past for that other familiar attitude: "Socialism is slavery. Sir, it will never be." It is no longer a question of dialectics, theories, and dreams. There is no question about it. The revolution is a fact. It is here now. Seven million revolutionists, organized, working day and night, are preaching the revolution —that passionate gospel, the Brotherhood of Man. Not only is it a cold-blooded economic propaganda, but it is in essence a religious propaganda with a fervour in it of Paul and Christ. The capitalist class has been indicted. It has failed in its management and its management is to be taken away from it. Seven million men of the working-class say that they are going to get the rest of the working-class to join with them and take the management away. The revolution is here, now. Stop it who can.

SACRAMENTO RIVER., March 1905.

THE SOMNAMBULISTS

"'Tis only fools speak evil of the clay -
The very stars are made of clay like mine."

The mightiest and absurdest sleep-walker on the planet! Chained in the circle of his own imaginings, man is only too keen to forget his origin and to shame that flesh of his that bleeds like all flesh and that is good to eat. Civilization (which is part of the circle of his imaginings) has spread a veneer over the surface of the soft-shelled animal known as man. It is a very thin veneer; but so wonderfully is man constituted that he squirms on his bit of achievement and believes he is garbed in armour-plate.

Yet man to-day is the same man that drank from his enemy's skull in the dark German forests, that sacked cities, and stole his women from neighbouring clans like any howling aborigine. The flesh-and-blood body of man has not changed in the last several thousand years. Nor has his mind changed. There is no faculty of the mind of man to-day that did not exist in the minds of the men of long ago. Man has to-day no concept that is too wide and deep and abstract for the mind of Plato or Aristotle to grasp. Give to Plato or Aristotle the same fund of knowledge that man to-day has access to, and Plato and Aristotle would reason as profoundly as the man of to-day and would achieve very similar conclusions.

It is the same old animal man, smeared over, it is true, with a veneer, thin and magical, that makes him dream drunken dreams of self-exaltation and to sneer at the flesh and the blood of him beneath the smear. The raw animal crouching within him is like the earthquake monster pent in the crust of the earth. As he persuades himself against the latter till it arouses and shakes down a city, so does he persuade himself against the former until it shakes him out of his dreaming and he stands undisguised, a brute like any other brute.

Starve him, let him miss six meals, and see gape through the veneer the hungry maw of the animal beneath. Get between him and the female of his kind upon whom his mating instinct is bent, and see his eyes blaze like an angry cat's, hear in his throat the scream of wild stallions, and watch his fists clench like an orang-outang's. Maybe he will even beat his chest. Touch his silly vanity, which he exalts into high-sounding pride—call him a liar, and behold the red animal in him that makes a hand clutching that is quick like the tensing of a tiger's claw, or an eagle's talon, incarnate with desire to rip and tear.

It is not necessary to call him a liar to touch his vanity. Tell a plains Indian that he has failed to steal horses from the neighbouring tribe, or tell a man living in bourgeois society that he has failed to pay his bills at the neighbouring grocer's, and the results are the same. Each, plains Indian and bourgeois, is smeared with a slightly different veneer, that is all. It requires a slightly different stick to scrape it off. The raw animals beneath are identical.

But intrude not violently upon man, leave him alone in his somnambulism, and he kicks out from under his feet the ladder of life up which he has climbed, constitutes himself the centre of the universe, dreams sordidly about his own particular god, and maunders metaphysically about his own blessed immortality.

True, he lives in a real world, breathes real air, eats real food, and sleeps under real blankets, in order to keep real cold away.

And there's the rub. He has to effect adjustments with the real world and at the same time maintain the sublimity of his dream. The result of this admixture of the real and the unreal is confusion thrice confounded. The man that walks the real world in his sleep becomes such a tangled mass of contradictions, paradoxes, and lies that he has to lie to himself in order to stay asleep.

In passing, it may be noted that some men are remarkably constituted in this matter of self-deception. They excel at deceiving themselves. They believe, and they help others to believe. It becomes their function in society, and some of them are paid large salaries for helping their fellow-men to believe, for instance, that they are not as other animals; for helping the king to believe, and his parasites and drudges as well, that he is God's own manager over so many square miles of earth-crust; for helping the merchant and banking classes to believe that society rests on their shoulders, and that civilization would go to smash if they got out from under and ceased from their exploitations and petty pilferings.

Prize-fighting is terrible. This is the dictum of the man who walks in his sleep. He prates about it, and writes to the papers about it, and worries the legislators about it. There is nothing of the brute about HIM. He is a sublimated soul that treads the heights and breathes refined ether—in self-comparison with the prize-fighter. The man who walks in his sleep ignores the flesh and all its wonderful play of muscle, joint, and nerve. He feels that there is something godlike in the mysterious deeps of his being, denies his relationship with the brute, and proceeds to go forth into the world and express by deeds that something godlike within him.

He sits at a desk and chases dollars through the weeks and months and years of his life. To him the life godlike resolves into a problem something like this: SINCE THE GREAT MASS OF MEN TOIL AT PRODUCING WEALTH, HOW BEST CAN HE GET BETWEEN THE GREAT MASS OF MEN AND THE WEALTH THEY PRODUCE,

AND GET A SLICE FOR HIMSELF? With tremendous exercise of craft, deceit, and guile, he devotes his life godlike to this purpose. As he succeeds, his somnambulism grows profound. He bribes legislatures, buys judges, "controls" primaries, and then goes and hires other men to tell him that it is all glorious and right. And the funniest thing about it is that this arch-deceiver believes all that they tell him. He reads only the newspapers and magazines that tell him what he wants to be told, listens only to the biologists who tell him that he is the finest product of the struggle for existence, and herds only with his own kind, where, like the monkey-folk, they teeter up and down and tell one another how great they are.

In the course of his life godlike he ignores the flesh—until he gets to table. He raises his hands in horror at the thought of the brutish prize-fighter, and then sits down and gorges himself on roast beef, rare and red, running blood under every sawing thrust of the implement called a knife. He has a piece of cloth which he calls a napkin, with which he wipes from his lips, and from the hair on his lips, the greasy juices of the meat.

He is fastidiously nauseated at the thought of two prize-fighters bruising each other with their fists; and at the same time, because it will cost him some money, he will refuse to protect the machines in his factory, though he is aware that the lack of such protection every year mangles, batters, and destroys out of all humanness thousands of working-men, women, and children. He will chatter about things refined and spiritual and godlike like himself, and he and the men who herd with him will calmly adulterate the commodities they put upon the market and which annually kill tens of thousands of babies and young children.

He will recoil at the suggestion of the horrid spectacle of two men confronting each other with gloved hands in the roped arena, and at the same time he will clamour for larger armies and larger navies, for more destructive war machines, which, with a single discharge, will disrupt and rip to pieces more human beings than have died in the whole history of prize-fighting. He will bribe a city council for a franchise or a state legislature for a commercial privilege; but he has never been known, in all his sleep-walking history, to bribe any legislative body in order to achieve any moral end, such as, for instance, abolition of prize-fighting, child-labour laws, pure food bills, or old age pensions.

"Ah, but we do not stand for the commercial life," object the refined, scholarly, and professional men. They are also sleep-walkers. They do not stand for the commercial life, but neither do they stand against it with all their strength. They submit to it, to the brutality and carnage of it. They develop classical economists who announce that the only possible way for men and women to get food and shelter is by the existing method. They produce university professors, men who claim the role of teachers, and who at the same time claim that the austere ideal of learning is passionless pursuit of passionless intelligence. They serve the men who lead the commercial life, give to their sons somnambulistic educations, preach that sleep-walking is the only way to walk, and that the persons who walk otherwise are atavisms or anarchists. They paint pictures for the commercial men, write books for them, sing songs for them, act plays for them, and dose them with various drugs when their bodies have grown gross or dyspeptic from overeating and lack of exercise.

Then there are the good, kind somnambulists who don't prize-fight, who don't play the commercial game, who don't teach and preach somnambulism, who don't do anything except live on the dividends that are coined out of the wan, white fluid that runs in the veins of little children, out of mothers' tears, the blood of strong men, and the groans and sighs of the old. The receiver is as bad as the thief—ay, and the thief is finer than the receiver; he at least has the courage to run the risk. But the good, kind people who don't do anything won't believe this, and the assertion will make them angry—for a moment. They possess several magic phrases, which are like the incantations of a voodoo doctor driving devils away. The phrases that the good, kind people repeat to themselves and to one another sound like "abstinence," "temperance," "thrift," "virtue." Sometimes they say them backward, when they sound like "prodigality," "drunkenness," "wastefulness," and "immorality." They do not really know the meaning of these phrases, but they think they do, and that is all that is necessary for somnambulists. The calm repetition of such phrases invariably drives away the waking devils and lulls to slumber.

Our statesmen sell themselves and their country for gold. Our municipal servants and state legislators commit countless treasons. The world of graft! The world of betrayal! The world of somnambulism, whose exalted and sensitive citizens are outraged by the knockouts of the prize-ring, and who annually not merely knock out, but kill, thousands of babies and children by means of child labour and adulterated food. Far better to have the front of one's face pushed in by the fist of an honest prize-fighter than to have the lining of one's stomach corroded by the embalmed beef of a dishonest manufacturer.

In a prize-fight men are classed. A lightweight fights with a light-weight; he never fights with a heavy-weight, and foul blows are not allowed. Yet in the world of the somnambulists, where soar the sublimated spirits, there are no classes, and foul blows are continually struck and never disallowed. Only they are not called foul blows. The world of claw and fang and fist and club has passed away—so say the somnambulists. A rebate is not an elongated claw. A Wall Street raid is not a fang slash. Dummy boards of directors and fake accountings are not foul blows of the fist under the belt. A present of coal stock by a mine operator to a railroad official is not a claw rip to the bowels of a rival mine operator. The hundred million dollars with which a combination beats down to his knees a man with a million dollars is not a club. The man who walks in his sleep says it is not a club. So say all of his kind with which he herds. They gather together and solemnly and gloatingly make and repeat certain noises that sound like "discretion," "acumen," "initiative," "enterprise." These noises are especially gratifying when they are made backward. They mean the same things, but they sound different. And in either case, forward or backward, the spirit of the dream is not disturbed.

When a man strikes a foul blow in the prize-ring the fight is immediately stopped, he is declared the loser, and he is hissed by the audience as he leaves the ring. But when a man who walks in his sleep strikes a foul blow he is immediately declared the victor and awarded the prize; and amid acclamations he forthwith turns his prize into a seat in the United States Senate, into a grotesque palace on Fifth Avenue, and into endowed churches, universities and libraries, to say nothing of subsidized newspapers, to proclaim his greatness.

The red animal in the somnambulist will out. He decries the carnal combat of the prize-ring, and compels the red animal to spiritual combat. The poisoned lie, the nasty, gossiping tongue, the brutality of the unkind epigram, the business and social nastiness and treachery of to-day—these are the thrusts and scratches of the red animal when the somnambulist is in charge. They are not the upper cuts and short arm jabs and jolts and slugging blows of the spirit. They are the foul blows of the spirit that have never been disbarred, as the foul blows of the prize-ring have been disbarred. (Would it not be preferable for a man to strike one full on the mouth with his fist than for him to tell a lie about one, or malign those that are nearest and dearest?)

For these are the crimes of the spirit, and, alas! they are so much more frequent than blows on the mouth. And whosoever exalts the spirit over the flesh, by his own creed avers that a crime of the spirit is vastly more terrible than a crime of the flesh. Thus stand the somnambulists convicted by their own creed—only they are not real men, alive and awake, and they proceed to mutter magic phrases that dispel all doubt as to their undiminished and eternal gloriousness.

It is well enough to let the ape and tiger die, but it is hardly fair to kill off the natural and courageous apes and tigers and allow the spawn of cowardly apes and tigers to live. The prize-fighting apes and tigers will die all in good time in the course of natural evolution, but they will not die so long as the cowardly, somnambulistic apes and tigers club and scratch and slash. This is not a brief for the prize-fighter. It is a blow of the fist between the eyes of the somnambulists, teetering up and down, muttering magic phrases, and thanking God that they are not as other animals.

GLEN ELLEN, CALIFORNIA., June 1900.

THE DIGNITY OF DOLLARS

Man is a blind, helpless creature. He looks back with pride upon his goodly heritage of the ages, and yet obeys unwittingly every mandate of that heritage; for it is incarnate with him, and in it are embedded the deepest roots of his soul. Strive as he will, he cannot escape it—unless he be a genius, one of those rare creations to whom alone is granted the privilege of doing entirely new and original things in entirely new and original ways. But the common clay-born man, possessing only talents, may do only what has been done before him. At the best, if he work hard, and cherish himself exceedingly, he may duplicate any or all previous performances of his kind; he may even do some of them better; but there he stops, the composite hand of his whole ancestry bearing heavily upon him.

And again, in the matter of his ideas, which have been thrust upon him, and which he has been busily garnering from the great world ever since the day when his eyes first focussed and he drew, startled, against the warm breast of his mother—the tyranny of these he cannot shake off. Servants of his will, they at the same time master him. They may not coerce genius, but they dictate and sway every action of the clay-born. If he hesitate on the verge of a new departure, they whip him back into the well-greased groove; if he pause, bewildered, at sight of some unexplored domain, they rise like ubiquitous finger-posts and direct him by the village path to the communal meadow. And he permits these things, and continues to permit them, for he cannot help them, and he is a slave. Out of his ideas he may weave cunning theories, beautiful ideals; but he is working with ropes of sand. At the slightest stress, the last least bit of cohesion flits away, and each idea flies apart from its fellows, while all clamour that he do this thing, or think this thing, in the ancient and time-honoured way. He is only a clay-born; so he bends his neck. He knows further that the clay-born are a pitiful, pitiless majority, and that he may do nothing which they do not do.

It is only in some way such as this that we may understand and explain the dignity which attaches itself to dollars. In the watches of the night, we may assure ourselves that there is no such dignity; but jostling with our fellows in the white light of day, we find that it does exist, and that we ourselves measure ourselves by the dollars we happen to possess. They give us confidence and carriage and dignity—ay, a personal dignity which goes down deeper than the garments with which we hide our nakedness. The world, when it knows nothing else of him, measures a man by his clothes; but the man himself, if he be neither a genius nor a philosopher, but merely a clay-born, measures himself by his pocket-book. He cannot help it, and can no more fling it from him than can the bashful young man his self-consciousness when crossing a ballroom floor.

I remember once absenting myself from civilization for weary months. When I returned, it was to a strange city in another country. The people were but slightly removed from my own breed, and they spoke the same tongue, barring a certain barbarous accent which I learned was far older than the one imbibed by me with my mother's milk. A fur cap, soiled and singed by many camp-fires, half sheltered the shaggy tendrils of my uncut hair. My foot-gear was of walrus hide, cunningly blended with seal gut. The remainder of my dress was as primal and uncouth. I was a sight to give merriment to gods and men. Olympus must have roared at my coming. The world, knowing me not, could judge me by my clothes alone. But I refused to be so judged. My spiritual backbone stiffened, and I held my head high, looking all men in the eyes. And I did these things, not that I was an egotist, not that I was impervious to the critical glances of my fellows, but because of a certain hogskin belt, plethoric and sweat-bewrinkled, which buckled next the skin above the hips. Oh, it's absurd, I grant, but had that belt not been so circumstanced, and so situated, I should have shrunk away into side streets and back alleys, walking humbly and avoiding all gregarious humans except those who were likewise abroad without belts. Why? I do not know, save that in such way did my fathers before me.

Viewed in the light of sober reason, the whole thing was preposterous. But I walked down the gang-plank with the mien of a hero, of a barbarian who knew himself to be greater than the civilization he invaded. I was possessed of the arrogance of a Roman governor. At last I knew what it was to be born to the purple, and I took my seat in the hotel carriage as though it were my chariot about to proceed with me to the imperial palace. People discreetly dropped their eyes before my proud gaze, and into their hearts I know I forced the query, What manner of man can this mortal be? I was superior to convention, and the very garb which otherwise would have damned me tended toward my elevation. And all this was due, not to my royal lineage, nor to the deeds I had done and the champions I had overthrown, but to a certain hogskin belt buckled next the skin. The sweat of months was upon it, toil had defaced it, and it was not a creation such as would appeal to the aesthetic mind; but it was plethoric. There was the arcanum; each yellow grain conduced to my exaltation, and the sum of these grains was the sum of my mightiness. Had they been less, just so would have been my stature; more, and I should have reached the sky.

And this was my royal progress through that most loyal city. I purchased a host of things from the tradespeople, and bought me such pleasures and diversions as befitted one who had long been denied. I scattered my gold lavishly, nor did I chaffer over prices in mart or exchange. And, because of these things I did, I demanded homage. Nor was it refused. I moved through wind-swept groves of limber backs; across sunny glades, lighted by the beaming rays from a thousand obsequious eyes; and when I tired of this, basked on the greensward of popular approval. Money was very good, I thought, and for the time was content. But there rushed upon me the words of Erasmus, "When I get some money I shall buy me some Greek books, and afterwards some clothes," and a great shame wrapped me around. But, luckily for my soul's welfare, I reflected and was saved. By the clearer vision vouchsafed me, I beheld Erasmus, fire-flashing, heaven-born, while I—I was merely a clay-born, a son of earth. For a giddy moment I had forgotten this, and tottered. And I rolled over on my greensward, caught a glimpse of a regiment of undulating backs, and thanked my particular gods that such moods of madness were passing brief.

But on another day, receiving with kingly condescension the service of my good subjects' backs, I remembered the words of another man, long since laid away, who was by birth a nobleman, by nature a philosopher and a gentleman, and who by circumstance yielded up his head upon the block. "That a man of lead," he once remarked, "who has no more sense than a log of wood, and is as bad as he is foolish, should have many wise and good men to serve him, only because he has a great heap of that metal; and that if, by some accident or trick of law (which sometimes produces as great changes as chance itself), all this wealth should pass from the master to the meanest varlet of his whole family, he himself would very soon become one of his servants, as if he were a thing that belonged to his wealth, and so was bound to follow its fortune."

And when I had remembered this much, I unwisely failed to pause and reflect. So I gathered my belongings together, cinched my hogskin belt tight about me, and went away to my own country. It was a very foolish thing to do. I am sure it was. But when I had recovered my reason, I fell upon my particular gods and berated them mightily, and as penance for their watchlessness placed them away amongst dust and cobwebs. Oh no, not for long. They are again enshrined, as bright and polished as of yore, and my destiny is once more in their keeping.

It is given that travail and vicissitude mark time to man's

footsteps as he stumbles onward toward the grave; and it is well. Without the bitter one may not know the sweet. The other day—nay, it was but yesterday—I fell before the rhythm of fortune. The inexorable pendulum had swung the counter direction, and there was upon me an urgent need. The hogskin belt was flat as famine, nor did it longer gird my loins. From my window I could descry, at no great distance, a very ordinary mortal of a man, working industriously among his cabbages. I thought: Here am I, capable of teaching him much concerning the field wherein he labours—the nitrogenic—why of the fertilizer, the alchemy of the sun, the microscopic cell-structure of the plant, the cryptic chemistry of root and runner—but thereat he straightened his work-wearied back and rested. His eyes wandered over what he had produced in the sweat of his brow, then on to mine. And as he stood there drearily, he became reproach incarnate. "Unstable as water," he said (I am sure he did)—"unstable as water, thou shalt not excel. Man, where are YOUR cabbages?"

I shrank back. Then I waxed rebellious. I refused to answer the question. He had no right to ask it, and his presence was an affront upon the landscape. And a dignity entered into me, and my neck was stiffened, my head poised. I gathered together certain certificates of goods and chattels, pointed my heel towards him and his cabbages, and journeyed townward. I was yet a man. There was naught in those certificates to be ashamed of. But alack-a-day! While my heels thrust the cabbage-man beyond the horizon, my toes were drawing me, faltering, like a timid old beggar, into a roaring spate of humanity-men, women, and children without end. They had no concern with me, nor I with them. I knew it; I felt it. Like She, after her fire- bath in the womb of the world, I dwindled in my own sight. My feet were uncertain and heavy, and my soul became as a meal sack, limp with emptiness and tied in the middle. People looked upon me scornfully, pitifully, reproachfully. (I can swear they did.) In every eye I read the question, Man, where are your cabbages?

So I avoided their looks, shrinking close to the kerbstone and by furtive glances directing my progress. At last I came hard by the place, and peering stealthily to the right and left that none who knew might behold me, I entered hurriedly, in the manner of one committing an abomination. 'Fore God! I had done no evil, nor had I wronged any man, nor did I contemplate evil; yet was I aware of evil. Why? I do not know, save that there goes much dignity with dollars, and being devoid of the one I was destitute of the other. The person I sought practised a profession as ancient as the oracles but far more lucrative. It is mentioned in Exodus; so it must have been created soon after the foundations of the world; and despite the thunder of ecclesiastics and the mailed hand of kings and conquerors, it has endured even to this day. Nor is it unfair to presume that the accounts of this most remarkable business will not be closed until the Trumps of Doom are sounded and all things brought to final balance.

Wherefore it was in fear and trembling, and with great modesty of spirit, that I entered the Presence. To confess that I was shocked were to do my feelings an injustice. Perhaps the blame may be shouldered upon Shylock, Fagin, and their ilk; but I had conceived an entirely different type of individual. This man—why, he was clean to look at, his eyes were blue, with the tired look of scholarly lucubrations, and his skin had the normal pallor of sedentary existence. He was reading a book, sober and leather-bound, while on his finely moulded, intellectual head reposed a black skull-cap. For all the world his look and attitude were those of a college professor. My heart gave a great leap. Here was hope! But no; he fixed me with a cold and glittering eye, searching with the chill of space till my financial status stood before him shivering and ashamed. I communed with myself: By his brow he is a thinker, but his intellect has been prostituted to a mercenary exaction of toll from misery. His nerve centres of judgment and will have not been employed in solving the problems of life, but in maintaining his own solvency by the insolvency of others. He trades upon sorrow and draws a livelihood from misfortune. He transmutes tears into treasure, and from nakedness and hunger garbs himself in clean linen and develops the round of his belly. He is a bloodsucker and a vampire. He lays unholy hands on heaven and hell at cent. per cent., and his very existence is a sacrilege and a blasphemy. And yet here am I, wilting before him, an arrant coward, with no respect for him and less for myself. Why should this shame be? Let me rouse in my strength and smite him, and, by so doing, wipe clean one offensive page.

But no. As I said, he fixed me with a cold and glittering eye, and in it was the aristocrat's undisguised contempt for the canaille. Behind him was the solid phalanx of a bourgeois society. Law and order upheld him, while I titubated, cabbageless, on the ragged edge. Moreover, he was possessed of a formula whereby to extract juice from a flattened lemon, and he would do business with me.

I told him my desires humbly, in quavering syllables. In return, he craved my antecedents and residence, pried into my private life, insolently demanded how many children had I and did I live in wedlock, and asked divers other unseemly and degrading questions. Ay, I was treated like a thief convicted before the act, till I produced my certificates of goods and chattels aforementioned. Never had they appeared so insignificant and paltry as then, when he sniffed over them with the air of one disdainfully doing a disagreeable task. It is said, "Thou shalt not lend upon usury to thy brother; usury of money, usury of victuals, usury of anything that is lent upon usury"; but he evidently was not my brother, for he demanded seventy per cent. I put my signature to certain indentures, received my pottage, and fled from his presence.

Faugh! I was glad to be quit of it. How good the outside air was! I only prayed that neither my best friend nor my worst enemy should ever become aware of what had just transpired. Ere I had gone a block I noticed that the sun had brightened perceptibly, the street become less sordid, the gutter mud less filthy. In people's eyes the cabbage question no longer brooded. And there was a spring to my body, an elasticity of step as I covered the pavement. Within me coursed an unwonted sap, and I felt as though I were about to burst out into leaves and buds and green things. My brain was clear and refreshed. There was a new strength to my arm. My nerves were tingling and I was a-pulse with the times. All men were my brothers. Save one—yes, save one. I would go back and wreck the establishment. I would disrupt that leather-bound volume, violate that black skullcap, burn the accounts. But before fancy could father the act, I recollected myself and all which had passed. Nor did I marvel at my new-horn might, at my ancient dignity which had returned. There was a tinkling chink as I ran the yellow pieces through my fingers, and with the golden music rippling round me I caught a deeper insight into the mystery of things.

OAKLAND, CALIFORNIA., February 1900.

GOLIAH

In 1924—to be precise, on the morning of January 3—the city of San Francisco awoke to read in one of its daily papers a curious letter, which had been received by Walter Bassett and which had evidently been written by some crank. Walter Bassett was the greatest captain of industry west of the Rockies, and was one of the small group that controlled the nation in everything but name. As such, he was the recipient of lucubrations from countless cranks; but this particular lucubration was so different from the average ruck of similar letters that, instead of putting it into the waste-basket, he had turned it over to a reporter. It was signed "Goliah," and the superscription gave his address as "Palgrave Island." The letter was as follows:

"MR. WALTER BASSETT,

"DEAR SIR:

"I am inviting you, with nine of your fellow-captains of industry, to visit me here on my island for the purpose of considering plans for the reconstruction of society upon a more rational basis. Up to the present, social evolution has been a blind and aimless, blundering thing. The time has come for a change. Man has risen from the vitalized slime of the primeval sea to the mastery of matter; but he has not yet mastered society. Man is to-day as much the slave to his collective stupidity, as a hundred thousand generations ago he was a slave to matter.

"There are two theoretical methods whereby man may become the master of society, and make of society an intelligent and efficacious device for the pursuit and capture of happiness and laughter. The first theory advances the proposition that no government can be wiser or better than the people that compose that government; that reform and development must spring from the individual; that in so far as the individuals become wiser and better, by that much will their government become wiser and better; in short, that the majority of individuals must become wiser and better, before their government becomes wiser and better. The mob, the political convention, the abysmal brutality and stupid ignorance of all concourses of people, give the lie to this theory. In a mob the collective intelligence and mercy is that of the least intelligent and most brutal members that compose the mob. On the other hand, a thousand passengers will surrender themselves to the wisdom and discretion of the captain, when their ship is in a storm on the sea. In such matter, he is the wisest and most experienced among them.

"The second theory advances the proposition that the majority of the people are not pioneers, that they are weighted down by the inertia of the established; that the government that is representative of them represents only their feebleness, and futility, and brutishness; that this blind thing called government is not the serf of their wills, but that they are the serfs of it; in short, speaking always of the great mass, that they do not make government, but that government makes them, and that government is and has been a stupid and awful monster, misbegotten of the glimmerings of intelligence that come from the inertia-crushed mass.

"Personally, I incline to the second theory. Also, I am impatient. For a hundred thousand generations, from the first social groups of our savage forbears, government has remained a monster. To-day, the inertia-crushed mass has less laughter in it than ever before. In spite of man's mastery of matter, human suffering and misery and degradation mar the fair world.

"Wherefore I have decided to step in and become captain of this world-ship for a while. I have the intelligence and the wide vision of the skilled expert. Also, I have the power. I shall be obeyed. The men of all the world shall perform my bidding and make governments so that they shall become laughter-producers. These modelled governments I have in mind shall not make the people happy, wise, and noble by decree; but they shall give opportunity for the people to become happy, wise, and noble.

"I have spoken. I have invited you, and nine of your fellow-captains, to confer with me. On March third the yacht Energon will sail from San Francisco. You are requested to be on board the night before. This is serious. The affairs of the world must be handled for a time by a strong hand. Mine is that strong hand. If you fail to obey my summons, you will die. Candidly, I do not expect that you will obey. But your death for failure to obey will cause obedience on the part of those I subsequently summon. You will have served a purpose. And please remember that I have no unscientific sentimentality about the value of human life. I carry always in the background of my consciousness the innumerable billions of lives that are to laugh and be happy in future aeons on the earth.

"Yours for the reconstruction of society,

"GOLIAH."

The publication of this letter did not cause even local amusement. Men might have smiled to themselves as they read it, but it was so palpably the handiwork of a crank that it did not merit discussion. Interest did not arouse till next morning. An Associated Press despatch to the Eastern states, followed by interviews by eager-nosed reporters, had brought out the names of the other nine captains of industry who had received similar letters, but who had not thought the matter of sufficient importance to be made public. But the interest aroused was mild, and it would have died out quickly had not

Gabberton cartooned a chronic presidential aspirant as "Goliah." Then came the song that was sung hilariously from sea to sea, with the refrain, "Goliah will catch you if you don't watch out."

The weeks passed and the incident was forgotten. Walter Bassett had forgotten it likewise; but on the evening of February 22, he was called to the telephone by the Collector of the Port. "I just wanted to tell you," said the latter, "that the yacht Energon has arrived and gone to anchor in the stream off Pier Seven."

What happened that night Walter Bassett has never divulged. But it is known that he rode down in his auto to the water front, chartered one of Crowley's launches, and was put aboard the strange yacht. It is further known that when he returned to the shore, three hours later, he immediately despatched a sheaf of telegrams to his nine fellow-captains of industry who had received letters from Goliah. These telegrams were similarly worded, and read: "The yacht Energon has arrived. There is something in this. I advise you to come."

Bassett was laughed at for his pains. It was a huge laugh that went up (for his telegrams had been made public), and the popular song on Goliah revived and became more popular than ever. Goliah and Bassett were cartooned and lampooned unmercifully, the former, as the Old Man of the Sea, riding on the latter's neck. The laugh tittered and rippled through clubs and social circles, was restrainedly merry in the editorial columns, and broke out in loud guffaws in the comic weeklies. There was a serious side as well, and Bassett's sanity was gravely questioned by many, and especially by his business associates.

Bassett had ever been a short-tempered man, and after he sent the second sheaf of telegrams to his brother captains, and had been laughed at again, he remained silent. In this second sheaf he had said: "Come, I implore you. As you value your life, come." He arranged all his business affairs for an absence, and on the night of March 2 went on board the Energon. The latter, properly cleared, sailed next morning. And next morning the newsboys in every city and town were crying "Extra."

In the slang of the day, Goliah had delivered the goods. The nine captains of industry who had failed to accept his invitation were dead. A sort of violent disintegration of the tissues was the report of the various autopsies held on the bodies of the slain millionaires; yet the surgeons and physicians (the most highly skilled in the land had participated) would not venture the opinion that the men had been slain. Much less would they venture the conclusion, "at the hands of parties unknown." It was all too mysterious. They were stunned. Their scientific credulity broke down. They had no warrant in the whole domain of science for believing that an anonymous person on Palgrave Island had murdered the poor gentlemen.

One thing was quickly learned, however; namely, that Palgrave Island was no myth. It was charted and well known to all navigators, lying on the line of 160 west longitude, right at its intersection by the tenth parallel north latitude, and only a few miles away from Diana Shoal. Like Midway and Fanning, Palgrave Island was isolated, volcanic and coral in formation. Furthermore, it was uninhabited. A survey ship, in 1887, had visited the place and reported the existence of several springs and of a good harbour that was very dangerous of approach. And that was all that was known of the tiny speck of land that was soon to have focussed on it the awed attention of the world.

Goliah remained silent till March 24. On the morning of that day, the newspapers published his second letter, copies of which had been received by the ten chief politicians of the United States—ten leading men in the political world who were conventionally known as "statesmen." The letter, with the same superscription as before, was as follows:

"DEAR SIR:

"I have spoken in no uncertain tone. I must be obeyed. You may consider this an invitation or a summons; but if you still wish to tread this earth and laugh, you will be aboard the yacht Energon, in San Francisco harbour, not later than the evening of April 5. It is my wish and my will that you confer with me here on Palgrave Island in the matter of reconstructing society upon some rational basis.

"Do not misunderstand me, when I tell you that I am one with a theory. I want to see that theory work, and therefore I call upon your cooperation. In this theory of mine, lives are but pawns; I deal with quantities of lives. I am after laughter, and those that stand in the way of laughter must perish. The game is big. There are fifteen hundred million human lives to-day on the planet. What is your single life against them? It is as naught, in my theory. And remember that mine is the power. Remember that I am a scientist, and that one life, or one million of lives, mean nothing to me as arrayed against the countless billions of billions of the lives of the generations to come. It is for their laughter that I seek to reconstruct society now; and against them your own meagre little life is a paltry thing indeed.

"Whoso has power can command his fellows. By virtue of that military device known as the phalanx, Alexander conquered his bit of the world. By virtue of that chemical device, gunpowder, Cortes with his several hundred cut-throats conquered the empire of the Montezumas. Now I am in possession of a device that is all my own. In the course of a century not more than half a dozen fundamental discoveries or inventions are made. I have made such an invention. The possession of it gives me the mastery of the world. I shall use this invention, not for commercial exploitation, but for the good of humanity. For that purpose I want help—willing agents, obedient hands; and I am strong enough to compel the service. I am taking the shortest way, though I am in no hurry. I shall not clutter my speed with haste.

"The incentive of material gain developed man from the savage to the semi-barbarian he is today. This incentive has been a useful device for the development of the human; but it has now fulfilled its function and is ready to be cast aside into the scrap-heap of rudimentary vestiges such as gills in the throat and belief in the divine right of kings. Of course you do not think so; but I do not see that that will prevent you from aiding me to fling the anachronism into the scrap-heap. For I tell you now that the time has come when mere food and shelter and similar sordid things shall be automatic, as free and easy and involuntary of access as the air. I shall make them automatic, what of my discovery and the power that discovery gives me. And with food and shelter automatic, the incentive of material gain passes away from the world for ever. With food and shelter automatic, the higher incentives will universally obtain—the spiritual, aesthetic, and intellectual incentives that will tend to develop and make beautiful and noble body, mind, and spirit. Then all the world will be dominated by happiness and laughter. It will be the reign of universal laughter.

"Yours for that day,

"GOLIAH."

Still the world would not believe. The ten politicians were at Washington, so that they did not have the opportunity of being convinced that Bassett had had, and not one of them took the trouble to journey out to San Francisco to make the opportunity. As for Goliah, he was hailed by the newspapers as another Tom Lawson with a panacea; and there were specialists in mental disease who, by analysis of Goliah's letters, proved conclusively that he was a lunatic.

The yacht Energon arrived in the harbour of San Francisco on the afternoon of April 5, and Bassett came ashore. But the Energon did not sail next day, for not one of the ten summoned politicians had elected to make the journey to

Palgrave Island. The newsboys, however, called "Extra" that day in all the cities. The ten politicians were dead. The yacht, lying peacefully at anchor in the harbour, became the centre of excited interest. She was surrounded by a flotilla of launches and rowboats, and many tugs and steamboats ran excursions to her. While the rabble was firmly kept off, the proper authorities and even reporters were permitted to board her. The mayor of San Francisco and the chief of police reported that nothing suspicious was to be seen upon her, and the port authorities announced that her papers were correct and in order in every detail. Many photographs and columns of descriptive matter were run in the newspapers.

The crew was reported to be composed principally of Scandinavians—fair-haired, blue-eyed Swedes, Norwegians afflicted with the temperamental melancholy of their race, stolid Russian Finns, and a slight sprinkling of Americans and English. It was noted that there was nothing mercurial and flyaway about them. They seemed weighty men, oppressed by a sad and stolid bovine-sort of integrity. A sober seriousness and enormous certitude characterized all of them. They appeared men without nerves and without fear, as though upheld by some overwhelming power or carried in the hollow of some superhuman hand. The captain, a sad-eyed, strong-featured American, was cartooned in the papers as "Gloomy Gus" (the pessimistic hero of the comic supplement).

Some sea-captain recognized the Energon as the yacht Scud, once owned by Merrivale of the New York Yacht Club. With this clue it was soon ascertained that the Scud had disappeared several years before. The agent who sold her reported the purchaser to be merely another agent, a man he had seen neither before nor since. The yacht had been reconstructed at Duffey's Shipyard in New Jersey. The change in her name and registry occurred at that time and had been legally executed. Then the Energon had disappeared in the shroud of mystery.

In the meantime, Bassett was going crazy—at least his friends and business associates said so. He kept away from his vast business enterprises and said that he must hold his hands until the other masters of the world could join with him in the reconstruction of society—proof indubitable that Goliah's bee had entered his bonnet. To reporters he had little to say. He was not at liberty, he said, to relate what he had seen on Palgrave Island; but he could assure them that the matter was serious, the most serious thing that had ever happened. His final word was that, the world was on the verge of a turnover, for good or ill he did not know, but, one way or the other, he was absolutely convinced that the turnover was coming. As for business, business could go hang. He had seen things, he had, and that was all there was to it.

There was a great telegraphing, during this period, between the local Federal officials and the state and war departments at Washington. A secret attempt was made late one afternoon to board the Energon and place the captain under arrest—the Attorney-General having given the opinion that the captain could be held for the murder of the ten "statesmen." The government launch was seen to leave Meigg's Wharf and steer for the Energon, and that was the last ever seen of the launch and the men on board of it. The government tried to keep the affair hushed up, but the cat was slipped out of the bag by the families of the missing men, and the papers were filled with monstrous versions of the affair.

The government now proceeded to extreme measures. The battleship Alaska was ordered to capture the strange yacht, or, failing that, to sink her. These were secret instructions; but thousands of eyes, from the water front and from the shipping in the harbour, witnessed what happened that afternoon. The battleship got under way and steamed slowly toward the Energon. At half a mile distant the battleship blew up—simply blew up, that was all, her shattered frame sinking to the bottom of the bay, a riff-raff of wreckage and a few survivors strewing the surface. Among the survivors was a young lieutenant who had had charge of the wireless on board the Alaska. The reporters got hold of him first, and he talked. No sooner had the Alaska got under way, he said, than a message was received from the Energon. It was in the international code, and it was a warning to the Alaska to come no nearer than half a mile. He had sent the message, through the speaking tube, immediately to the captain. He did not know anything more, except that the Energon twice repeated the message and that five minutes afterward the explosion occurred. The captain of the Alaska had perished with his ship, and nothing more was to be learned.

The Energon, however, promptly hoisted anchor and cleared out to sea. A great clamour was raised by the papers; the government was charged with cowardice and vacillation in its dealings with a mere pleasure yacht and a lunatic who called himself "Goliah," and immediate and decisive action was demanded. Also, a great cry went up about the loss of life, especially the wanton killing of the ten "statesmen." Goliah promptly replied. In fact, so prompt was his reply that the experts in wireless telegraphy announced that, since it was impossible to send wireless messages so great a distance, Goliah was in their very midst and not on Palgrave Island. Goliah's letter was delivered to the Associated Press by a messenger boy who had been engaged on the street. The letter was as follows:

"What are a few paltry lives? In your insane wars you destroy millions of lives and think nothing of it. In your fratricidal commercial struggle you kill countless babes, women, and men, and you triumphantly call the shambles 'individualism.' I call it anarchy. I am going to put a stop to your wholesale destruction of human beings. I want laughter, not slaughter. Those of you who stand in the way of laughter will get slaughter.

"Your government is trying to delude you into believing that the destruction of the Alaska was an accident. Know here and now that it was by my orders that the Alaska was destroyed. In a few short months, all battleships on all seas will be destroyed or flung to the scrap-heap, and all nations shall disarm; fortresses shall be dismantled, armies disbanded, and warfare shall cease from the earth. Mine is the power. I am the will of

God. The whole world shall be in vassalage to me, but it shall be a vassalage of peace.

"I am

GOLIAH."

"Blow Palgrave Island out of the water!" was the head-line retort of the newspapers. The government was of the same frame of mind, and the assembling of the fleets began. Walter Bassett broke out in ineffectual protest, but was swiftly silenced by the threat of a lunacy commission. Goliah remained silent. Against Palgrave Island five great fleets were hurled—the Asiatic Squadron, the South Pacific Squadron, the North Pacific Squadron, the Caribbean Squadron, and half of the North Atlantic Squadron, the two latter coming through the Panama Canal.

"I have the honour to report that we sighted Palgrave Island on the evening of April 29," ran the report of Captain Johnson, of the battleship North Dakota, to the Secretary of the Navy. "The Asiatic Squadron was delayed and did not arrive until the morning of April 30. A council of the admirals was held, and it was decided to attack early next morning. The destroyer, Swift VII, crept in, unmolested, and reported no warlike preparations on the island. It noted several small merchant steamers in the harbour, and the existence of a small village in a hopelessly exposed position that could be swept by our fire.

"It had been decided that all the vessels should rush in, scattered, upon the island, opening fire at three miles, and continuing to the edge of the reef, there to retain loose formation and engage. Palgrave Island repeatedly warned us, by wireless, in the international code, to keep outside the ten-mile limit; but no heed was paid to the warnings.

"The North Dakota did not take part in the movement of the morning of May 1. This was due to a slight accident of the preceding night that temporarily disabled her steering-gear. The morning of May 1 broke clear and calm. There was a slight breeze from the south-west that quickly died away. The North Dakota lay twelve miles off the island. At the signal the squadrons charged in upon the island, from all sides, at full speed. Our wireless receiver continued to tick off warnings from the island. The ten-mile limit was passed, and nothing happened. I watched through my glasses. At five miles nothing happened; at four miles nothing happened; at three miles, the New York, in the lead on our side of the island, opened fire. She fired only one shot. Then she blew up. The rest of the vessels never fired a shot. They began to blow up, everywhere, before our eyes. Several swerved about and started back, but they failed to escape. The destroyer, Dart XXX, nearly made the ten-mile limit when she blew up. She was the last survivor. No harm came to the North Dakota, and that night, the steering-gear being repaired, I gave orders to sail for San Francisco."

To say that the United States was stunned is but to expose the inadequacy of language. The whole world was stunned. It confronted that blight of the human brain, the unprecedented. Human endeavour was a jest, a monstrous futility, when a lunatic on a lonely island, who owned a yacht and an exposed village, could destroy five of the proudest fleets of Christendom. And how had he done it? Nobody knew. The scientists lay down in the dust of the common road and wailed and gibbered. They did not know. Military experts committed suicide by scores. The mighty fabric of warfare they had fashioned was a gossamer veil rent asunder by a miserable lunatic. It was too much for their sanity. Mere human reason could not withstand the shock. As the savage is crushed by the sleight-of-hand of the witch doctor, so was the world crushed by the magic of Goliah. How did he do it? It was the awful face of the Unknown upon which the world gazed and by which it was frightened out of the memory of its proudest achievements.

But all the world was not stunned. There was the invariable

exception—the Island Empire of Japan. Drunken with the wine of success deep-quaffed, without superstition and without faith in aught but its own ascendant star, laughing at the wreckage of science and mad with pride of race, it went forth upon the way of war. America's fleets had been destroyed. From the battlements of heaven the multitudinous ancestral shades of Japan leaned down. The opportunity, God-given, had come. The Mikado was in truth a brother to the gods.

The war-monsters of Japan were loosed in mighty fleets. The Philippines were gathered in as a child gathers a nosegay. It took longer for the battleships to travel to Hawaii, to Panama, and to the Pacific Coast. The United States was panic-stricken, and there arose the powerful party of dishonourable peace. In the midst of the clamour the Energon arrived in San Francisco Bay and Goliah spoke once more. There was a little brush as the Energon came in, and a few explosions of magazines occurred along the war-tunnelled hills as the coast defences went to smash. Also, the blowing up of the submarine mines in the Golden Gate made a remarkably fine display. Goliah's message to the people of San Francisco, dated as usual from Palgrave Island, was published in the papers. It ran:

"Peace? Peace be with you. You shall have peace. I have spoken to this purpose before. And give you me peace. Leave my yacht Energon alone. Commit one overt act against her and not one stone in San Francisco shall stand upon another.

"To-morrow let all good citizens go out upon the hills that slope down to the sea. Go with music and laughter and garlands. Make festival for the new age that is dawning. Be like children upon your hills, and witness the passing of war. Do not miss the opportunity. It is your last chance to behold what henceforth you will be compelled to seek in museums of antiquities.

"I promise you a merry day,

"GOLIAH."

The madness of magic was in the air. With the people it was as if all their gods had crashed and the heavens still stood. Order and law had passed away from the universe; but the sun still shone, the wind still blew, the flowers still bloomed—that was the amazing thing about it. That water should continue to run downhill was a miracle. All the stabilities of the human mind and human achievement were crumbling. The one stable thing that remained was Goliah, a madman on an island. And so it was that the whole population of San Francisco went forth next day in colossal frolic upon the hills that overlooked the sea. Brass bands and banners went forth, brewery wagons and Sunday-school picnics—all the strange heterogeneous groupings of swarming metropolitan life.

On the sea-rim rose the smoke from the funnels of a hundred hostile vessels of war, all converging upon the helpless, undefended Golden Gate. And not all undefended, for out through the Golden Gate moved the Energon, a tiny toy of white, rolling like a straw in the stiff sea on the bar where a strong ebb-tide ran in the teeth of the summer sea-breeze. But the Japanese were cautious. Their thirty-and forty-thousand-ton battleships slowed down half a dozen miles offshore and manoeuvred in ponderous evolutions, while tiny scout-boats (lean, six-funnelled destroyers) ran in, cutting blackly the flashing sea like so many sharks. But, compared with the Energon, they were leviathans. Compared with them, the Energon was as the sword of the arch-angel Michael, and they the forerunners of the hosts of hell.

But the flashing of the sword, the good people of San Francisco, gathered on her hills, never saw. Mysterious, invisible, it cleaved the air and smote the mightiest blows of combat the world had ever witnessed. The good people of San Francisco saw little and understood less. They saw only a million and a half tons of brine-cleaving, thunder-flinging fabrics hurled skyward and smashed back in ruin to sink into the sea. It was all over in five minutes. Remained upon the wide expanse of sea only the Energon, rolling white and toylike on the bar.

Goliah spoke to the Mikado and the Elder Statesmen. It was only an ordinary cable message, despatched from San Francisco by the captain of the Energon, but it was of sufficient moment to cause the immediate withdrawal of Japan from the Philippines and of her surviving fleets from the sea. Japan the sceptical was converted. She had felt the weight of Goliah's arm. And meekly she obeyed when Goliah commanded her to dismantle her war vessels and to turn the metal into useful appliances for the arts of peace. In all the ports, navy-yards, machine-shops, and foundries of Japan tens of thousands of brown-skinned artisans converted the war-monsters into myriads of useful things, such as ploughshares (Goliah insisted on ploughshares), gasolene engines, bridge-trusses, telephone and telegraph wires, steel rails, locomotives, and rolling stock for railways. It was a world-penance for a world to see, and paltry indeed it made appear that earlier penance, barefooted in the snow, of an emperor to a pope for daring to squabble over temporal power.

Goliah's next summons was to the ten leading scientists of the United States. This time there was no hesitancy in obeying. The savants were ludicrously prompt, some of them waiting in San Francisco for weeks so as not to miss the scheduled sailing-date. They departed on the Energon on June 15; and while they were on the sea, on the way to Palgrave Island, Goliah performed another spectacular feat. Germany and France were preparing to fly at each other's throats. Goliah commanded peace. They ignored the command, tacitly agreeing to fight it out on land where it seemed safer for the belligerently inclined. Goliah set the date of June 19 for the cessation of hostile preparations. Both countries mobilized their armies on June 18, and hurled them at the common frontier. And on June 19, Goliah struck. All generals, war-secretaries, and jingo-leaders in the two countries died on that day; and that day two vast armies, undirected, like strayed sheep, walked over each other's frontiers and fraternized. But the great German war lord had escaped—it was learned, afterward, by hiding in the huge safe where were stored the secret archives of his empire. And when he emerged he was a very penitent war lord, and like the

Mikado of Japan he was set to work beating his sword-blades into ploughshares and pruning-hooks.

But in the escape of the German Emperor was discovered a great significance. The scientists of the world plucked up courage, got back their nerve. One thing was conclusively evident—Goliah's power was not magic. Law still reigned in the universe. Goliah's power had limitations, else had the German Emperor not escaped by secretly hiding in a steel safe. Many learned articles on the subject appeared in the magazines.

The ten scientists arrived back from Palgrave Island on July 6. Heavy platoons of police protected them from the reporters. No, they had not see Goliah, they said in the one official interview that was vouchsafed; but they had talked with him, and they had seen things. They were not permitted to state definitely all that they had seen and heard, but they could say that the world was about to be revolutionized. Goliah was in the possession of a tremendous discovery that placed all the world at his mercy, and it was a good thing for the world that Goliah was merciful. The ten scientists proceeded directly to Washington on a special train, where, for days, they were closeted with the heads of government, while the nation hung breathless on the outcome.

But the outcome was a long time in arriving. From Washington the President issued commands to the masters and leading figures of the nation. Everything was secret. Day by day deputations of bankers, railway lords, captains of industry, and Supreme Court justices arrived; and when they arrived they remained. The weeks dragged on, and then, on August 25, began the famous issuance of proclamations. Congress and the Senate co-operated with the President in this, while the Supreme Court justices gave their sanction and the money lords and the captains of industry agreed. War was declared upon the capitalist masters of the nation. Martial law was declared over the whole United States. The supreme power was vested in the President.

In one day, child-labour in the whole country was abolished. It was done by decree, and the United States was prepared with its army to enforce its decrees. In the same day all women factory workers were dismissed to their homes, and all the sweat-shops were closed. "But we cannot make profits!" wailed the petty capitalists. "Fools!" was the retort of Goliah. "As if the meaning of life were profits! Give up your businesses and your profit-mongering." "But there is nobody to buy our business!" they wailed. "Buy and sell—is that all the meaning life has for you?" replied Goliah. "You have nothing to sell. Turn over your little cut-throating, anarchistic businesses to the government so that they may be rationally organized and operated." And the next day, by decree, the government began taking possession of all factories, shops, mines, ships, railroads, and producing lands.

The nationalization of the means of production and distribution went on apace. Here and there were sceptical capitalists of moment. They were made prisoners and haled to Palgrave Island, and when they returned they always acquiesced in what the government was doing. A little later the journey to Palgrave Island became unnecessary. When objection was made, the reply of the officials was "Goliah has spoken"— which was another way of saying, "He must be obeyed."

The captains of industry became heads of departments. It was found that civil engineers, for instance, worked just as well in government employ as before, they had worked in private employ. It was found that men of high executive ability could not violate their nature. They could not escape exercising their executive ability, any more than a crab could escape crawling or a bird could escape flying. And so it was that all the splendid force of the men who had previously worked for themselves was now put to work for the good of society. The half-dozen great railway chiefs co-operated in the organizing of a national system of railways that was amazingly efficacious. Never again was there such a thing as a car shortage. These chiefs were not the Wall Street railway magnates, but they were the men who formerly had done the real work while in the employ of the Wall Street magnates.

Wall Street was dead. There was no more buying and selling and speculating. Nobody had anything to buy or sell. There was nothing in which to speculate. "Put the stock gamblers to work," said Goliah; "give those that are young, and that so desire, a chance to learn useful trades." "Put the drummers, and salesmen, and advertising agents, and real estate agents to work," said Goliah; and by hundreds of thousands the erstwhile useless middlemen and parasites went into useful occupations. The four hundred thousand idle gentlemen of the country who had lived upon incomes were likewise put to work. Then there were a lot of helpless men in high places who were cleared out, the remarkable thing about this being that they were cleared out by their own fellows. Of this class were the professional politicians, whose wisdom and power consisted of manipulating machine politics and of grafting. There was no longer any graft. Since there were no private interests to purchase special privileges, no bribes were offered to legislators, and legislators for the first time legislated for the people. The result was that men who were efficient, not in corruption, but in direction, found their way into the legislatures.

With this rational organization of society amazing results were brought about. The national day's work was eight hours, and yet production increased. In spite of the great permanent improvements and of the immense amount of energy consumed in systematizing the competitive chaos of society, production doubled and tripled upon itself. The standard of living increased, and still consumption could not keep up with production. The maximum working age was decreased to fifty years, to forty-nine years, and to forty-eight years. The minimum working age went up from sixteen years to eighteen years. The eight-hour day became a seven-hour day, and in a few months the national working day was reduced to five hours.

In the meantime glimmerings were being caught, not of the

identity of Goliah, but of how he had worked and prepared for his assuming control of the world. Little things leaked out, clues were followed up, apparently unrelated things were pieced together. Strange stories of blacks stolen from Africa were remembered, of Chinese and Japanese contract coolies who had mysteriously disappeared, of lonely South Sea Islands raided and their inhabitants carried away; stories of yachts and merchant steamers, mysteriously purchased, that had disappeared and the descriptions of which remotely tallied with the crafts that had carried the Orientals and Africans and islanders away. Where had Goliah got the sinews of war? was the question. And the surmised answer was: By exploiting these stolen labourers. It was they that lived in the exposed village on Palgrave Island. It was the product of their toil that had purchased the yachts and merchant steamers and enabled Goliah's agents to permeate society and carry out his will. And what was the product of their toil that had given Goliah the wealth necessary to realize his plans? Commercial radium, the newspapers proclaimed; and radiyte, and radiosole, and argatium, and argyte, and the mysterious golyte (that had proved so valuable in metallurgy). These were the new compounds, discovered in the first decade of the twentieth century, the commercial and scientific use of which had become so enormous in the second decade.

The line of fruit boats that ran from Hawaii to San Francisco was declared to be the property of Goliah. This was a surmise, for no other owner could be discovered, and the agents who handled the shipments of the fruit boats were only agents. Since no one else owned the fruit boats, then Goliah must own them. The point of which is: THAT IT LEAKED OUT THAT THE MAJOR PORTION of THE WORLD'S SUPPLY IN THESE PRECIOUS COMPOUNDS WAS BROUGHT TO SAN FRANCISCO BY THOSE VERY FRUIT BOATS. That the whole chain of surmise was correct was proved in later years when Goliah's slaves were liberated and honourably pensioned by the international government of the world. It was at that time that the seal of secrecy was lifted from the lips of his agents and higher emissaries, and those that chose revealed much of the mystery of Goliah's organization and methods. His destroying angels, however, remained for ever dumb. Who the men were who went forth to the high places and killed at his bidding will be unknown to the end of time—for kill they did, by means of that very subtle and then-mysterious force that Goliah had discovered and named "Energon."

But at that time Energon, the little giant that was destined to do the work of the world, was unknown and undreamed of. Only Goliah knew, and he kept his secret well. Even his agents, who were armed with it, and who, in the case of the yacht Energon, destroyed a mighty fleet of war-ships by exploding their magazines, knew not what the subtle and potent force was, nor how it was manufactured. They knew only one of its many uses, and in that one use they had been instructed by Goliah. It is now well known that radium, and radiyte, and radiosole, and all the other compounds, were by-products of the manufacture of Energon by Goliah from the sunlight; but at that time nobody knew what Energon was, and Goliah continued to awe and rule the world.

One of the uses of Energon was in wireless telegraphy. It was by its means that Goliah was able to communicate with his agents all over the world. At that time the apparatus required by an agent was so clumsy that it could not be packed in anything less than a fair-sized steamer trunk. To-day, thanks to the improvements of Hendsoll, the perfected apparatus can be carried in a coat pocket.

It was in December, 1924, that Goliah sent out his famous "Christmas Letter," part of the text of which is here given:

"So far, while I have kept the rest of the nations from each other's throats, I have devoted myself particularly to the United States. Now I have not given to the people of the United States a rational social organization. What I have done has been to compel them to make that organization them-selves. There is more laughter in the United States these days, and there is more sense. Food and shelter are no longer obtained by the anarchistic methods of so-called individualism but are now wellnigh automatic. And the beauty of it is that the people of the United States have achieved all this for themselves. I did not achieve it for them. I repeat, they achieved it for themselves. All that I did was to put the fear of death in the hearts of the few that sat in the high places and obstructed the coming of rationality and laughter. The fear of death made those in the high places get out of the way, that was all, and gave the intelligence of man a chance to realize itself socially.

"In the year that is to come I shall devote myself to the rest of the world. I shall put the fear of death in the hearts of all that sit in the high places in all the nations. And they will do as they have done in the United States—get down out of the high places and give the intelligence of man a chance for social rationality. All the nations shall tread the path the United States is now on.

"And when all the nations are well along on that path, I shall have something else for them. But first they must travel that path for themselves. They must demonstrate that the intelligence of mankind to-day, with the mechanical energy now at its disposal, is capable of organizing society so that food and shelter be made automatic, labour be reduced to a three-hour day, and joy and laughter be made universal. And when that is accomplished, not by me but by the intelligence of mankind, then I shall make a present to the world of a new mechanical energy. This is my discovery. This Energon is nothing more nor less than the cosmic energy that resides in the solar rays. When it is harnessed by mankind it will do the work of the world. There will be no more multitudes of miners slaving out their lives in the bowels of the earth, no more sooty firemen and greasy engineers. All may dress in white if they so will. The work of life will have become play and young and old will be the children of joy, and the business of living will become joy; and they will compete, one with another, in achieving ethical concepts and spiritual heights, in fashioning pictures and songs, and stories, in statecraft and beauty craft, in the sweat and the endeavour of the wrestler and the runner and the player of games—all will compete, not for sordid coin and base material reward, but for the joy that shall be theirs in the development and vigour of flesh and in the development and keenness of spirit. All will be joy-smiths, and their task shall be to beat out laughter from the ringing anvil of life.

"And now one word for the immediate future. On New Year's Day all nations shall disarm, all fortresses and war-ships shall be dismantled, and all armies shall be disbanded.

GOLIAH."

On New Year's Day all the world disarmed. The millions of soldiers and sailors and workmen in the standing armies, in the navies, and in the countless arsenals, machine-shops, and factories for the manufacture of war machinery, were dismissed to their homes. These many millions of men, as well as their costly war machinery, had hitherto been supported on the back of labour. They now went into useful occupations, and the released labour giant heaved a mighty sigh of relief. The policing of the world was left to the peace officers and was purely social, whereas war had been distinctly anti-social.

Ninety per cent. of the crimes against society had been crimes against private property. With the passing of private property, at least in the means of production, and with the organization of industry that gave every man a chance, the crimes against private property practically ceased. The police forces everywhere were reduced repeatedly and again and again. Nearly all occasional and habitual criminals ceased voluntarily from their depredations. There was no longer any need for them to commit crime. They merely changed with changing conditions. A smaller number of criminals was put into hospitals and cured. And the remnant of the hopelessly criminal and degenerate was segregated. And the courts in all countries were likewise decreased in number again and again. Ninety-five per cent. of all civil cases had been squabbles over property, conflicts of property-rights, lawsuits, contests of wills, breaches of contract, bankruptcies, etc. With the passing of private property, this ninety-five per cent. of the cases that cluttered the courts also passed. The courts became shadows, attenuated ghosts, rudimentary vestiges of the anarchistic times that had preceded the coming of Goliah.

The year 1925 was a lively year in the world's history. Goliah ruled the world with a strong hand. Kings and emperors journeyed to Palgrave Island, saw the wonders of Energon, and went away, with the fear of death in their hearts, to abdicate thrones and crowns and hereditary licenses. When Goliah spoke to politicians (so-called "statesmen"), they obeyed . . . or died. He dictated universal reforms, dissolved refractory parliaments, and to the great conspiracy that was formed of mutinous money lords and captains of industry he sent his destroying angels. "The time is past for fooling," he told them. "You are anachronisms. You stand in the way of humanity. To the scrap-heap with you." To those that protested, and they were many, he said: "This is no time for logomachy. You can argue for centuries. It is what you have done in the past. I have no time for argument. Get out of the way."

With the exception of putting a stop to war, and of indicating the broad general plan, Goliah did nothing. By putting the fear of death into the hearts of those that sat in the high places and obstructed progress, Goliah made the opportunity for the unshackled intelligence of the best social thinkers of the world to exert itself. Goliah left all the multitudinous details of reconstruction to these social thinkers. He wanted them to prove that they were able to do it, and they proved it. It was due to their initiative that the white plague was stamped out from the world. It was due to them, and in spite of a deal of protesting from the sentimentalists, that all the extreme hereditary inefficients were segregated and denied marriage.

Goliah had nothing whatever to do with the instituting of the colleges of invention. This idea originated practically simultaneously in the minds of thousands of social thinkers. The time was ripe for the realization of the idea, and everywhere arose the splendid institutions of invention. For the first time the ingenuity of man was loosed upon the problem of simplifying life, instead of upon the making of money-earning devices. The affairs of life, such as house-cleaning, dish and window-washing, dust-removing, and scrubbing and clothes-washing, and all the endless sordid and necessary details, were simplified by invention until they became automatic. We of to-day cannot realize the barbarously filthy and slavish lives of those that lived prior to 1925.

The international government of the world was another idea that sprang simultaneously into the minds of thousands. The successful realization of this idea was a surprise to many, but as a surprise it was nothing to that received by the mildly protestant sociologists and biologists when irrefutable facts exploded the doctrine of Malthus. With leisure and joy in the world; with an immensely higher standard of living; and with the enormous spaciousness of opportunity for recreation, development, and pursuit of beauty and nobility and all the higher attributes, the birth-rate fell, and fell astoundingly. People ceased breeding like cattle. And better than that, it was immediately noticeable that a higher average of children was being born. The doctrine of Malthus was knocked into a cocked hat—or flung to the scrap-heap, as Goliah would have put it.

All that Goliah had predicted that the intelligence of mankind could accomplish with the mechanical energy at its disposal, came to pass. Human dissatisfaction practically disappeared. The elderly people were the great grumblers; but when they were honourably pensioned by society, as they passed the age limit for work, the great majority ceased grumbling. They found themselves better off in their idle old days under the new regime, enjoying vastly more pleasure and comforts than they had in their busy and toilsome youth under the old regime. The younger generation had easily adapted itself too the changed order, and the very young had never known anything else. The sum of human happiness had increased enormously. The world had become gay and sane. Even the old fogies of professors of sociology, who had opposed with might and main the coming of the new regime, made no complaint. They were a score of times better remunerated than in the old days, and they were not worked nearly so hard. Besides, they were busy revising sociology and writing new text-books on the subject. Here and there, it is true, there were atavisms, men who yearned for the flesh-pots and cannibal-feasts of the old alleged "individualism," creatures long of teeth and savage of claw who wanted to prey upon their fellow-men; but they were looked upon as diseased, and were treated in hospitals. A small remnant, however, proved incurable, and was confined in asylums and denied marriage. Thus there was no progeny to inherit their atavistic tendencies.

As the years went by, Goliah dropped out of the running of the world. There was nothing for him to run. The world was running itself, and doing it smoothly and beautifully. In 1937, Goliah made his long-promised present of Energon to the world. He himself had devised a thousand ways in which the little giant should do the work of the world—all of which he made public at the same time. But instantly the colleges of invention seized upon Energon and utilized it in a hundred thousand additional ways. In fact, as Goliah confessed in his letter of March 1938, the colleges of invention cleared up several puzzling features of Energon that had baffled him during the preceding years. With the introduction of the use of Energon the two-hour work-day was cut down almost to nothing. As Goliah had predicted, work indeed became play. And, so tremendous was man's productive capacity, due to Energon and the rational social utilization of it, that the humblest citizen enjoyed leisure and time and opportunity for an immensely greater abundance of living than had the most favoured under the old anarchistic system.

Nobody had ever seen Goliah, and all peoples began to clamour for their saviour to appear. While the world did not minimize his discovery of Energon, it was decided that greater than that was his wide social vision. He was a superman, a scientific superman; and the curiosity of the world to see him had become wellnigh unbearable. It was in 1941, after much hesitancy on his part, that he finally emerged from Palgrave Island. He arrived on June 6 in San Francisco, and for the first time, since his retirement to Palgrave Island, the world looked upon his face. And the world was disappointed. Its imagination had been touched. An heroic figure had been made out of Goliah. He was the man, or the demi-god, rather, who had turned the planet over. The deeds of Alexander, Caesar, Genghis Khan, and Napoleon were as the play of babes alongside his colossal achievements.

And ashore in San Francisco and through its streets stepped and rode a little old man, sixty-five years of age, well preserved, with a pink-and-white complexion and a bald spot on his head the size of an apple. He was short-sighted and wore spectacles. But when the spectacles were removed, his were quizzical blue eyes like a child's, filled with mild wonder at the world. Also his eyes had a way of twinkling, accompanied by a screwing up of the face, as if he laughed at the huge joke he had played upon the world, trapping it, in spite of itself, into happiness and laughter.

For a scientific superman and world tyrant, he had remarkable weaknesses. He loved sweets, and was inordinately fond of salted almonds and salted pecans, especially of the latter. He always carried a paper bag of them in his pocket, and he had a way of saying frequently that the chemism of his nature demanded such fare. Perhaps his most astonishing failing was cats. He had an ineradicable aversion to that domestic animal. It will be remembered that he fainted dead away with sudden fright, while speaking in Brotherhood Palace, when the janitor's cat walked out upon the stage and brushed against his legs.

But no sooner had he revealed himself to the world than he was identified. Old-time friends had no difficulty in recognizing him as Percival Stultz, the German-American who, in 1898, had worked in the Union Iron Works, and who, for two years at that time, had been secretary of Branch 369 of the International Brotherhood of Machinists. It was in 1901, then twenty-five years of age, that he had taken special scientific courses at the University of California, at the same time supporting himself by soliciting what was then known as "life insurance." His records as a student are preserved in the university museum, and they are unenviable. He is remembered by the professors he sat under chiefly for his absent-mindedness. Undoubtedly, even then, he was catching glimpses of the wide visions that later were to be his.

His naming himself "Goliah" and shrouding himself in mystery was his little joke, he later explained. As Goliah, or any other thing like that, he said, he was able to touch the imagination of the world and turn it over; but as Percival Stultz, wearing side-whiskers and spectacles, and weighing one hundred and eighteen pounds, he would have been unable to turn over a pecan—"not even a salted pecan."

But the world quickly got over its disappointment in his personal appearance and antecedents. It knew him and revered him as the master-mind of the ages; and it loved him for himself, for his quizzical short-sighted eyes and the inimitable way in which he screwed up his face when he laughed; it loved him for his simplicity and comradeship and warm humanness, and for his fondness for salted pecans and his aversion to cats. And to-day, in the wonder-city of Asgard, rises in awful beauty that monument to him that dwarfs the pyramids and all the monstrous blood-stained monuments of antiquity. And on that monument, as all know, is inscribed in imperishable bronze the prophecy and the fulfilment: "ALL WILL BE JOY-SMITHS, AND THEIR TASK SHALL BE TO BEAT OUT LAUGHTER FROM THE RINGING ANVIL OF LIFE."

[EDITORIAL NOTE.—This remarkable production is the work of Harry Beckwith, a student in the Lowell High School of San Francisco, and it is here reproduced chiefly because of the youth of its author. Far be it from our policy to burden our readers with ancient history; and when it is known that Harry Beckwith was only fifteen when the fore-going was written, our motive will be understood. "Goliah" won the Premier for high school composition in 2254, and last year Harry Beckwith took advantage of the privilege earned, by electing to spend six months in Asgard. The wealth of historical detail, the atmosphere of the times, and the mature style of the composition are especially noteworthy in one so young.]

THE GOLDEN POPPY

I have a poppy field. That is, by the grace of God and the good-nature of editors, I am enabled to place each month divers gold pieces into a clerical gentleman's hands, and in return for said gold pieces I am each month reinvested with certain proprietary-rights in a poppy field. This field blazes on the rim of the Piedmont Hills. Beneath lies all the world. In the distance, across the silver sweep of bay, San Francisco smokes on her many hills like a second Rome. Not far away, Mount Tamalpais thrusts a rugged shoulder into the sky; and midway between is the Golden Gate, where sea mists love to linger. From the poppy field we often see the shimmering blue of the Pacific beyond, and the busy ships that go for ever out and in.

"We shall have great joy in our poppy field," said Bess. "Yes," said I; "how the poor city folk will envy when they come to see us, and how we will make all well again when we send them off with great golden armfuls!"

"But those things will have to come down," I added, pointing to numerous obtrusive notices (relics of the last tenant) displayed conspicuously along the boundaries, and bearing, each and all, this legend:

"PRIVATE GROUNDS. NO TRESPASSING."

"Why should we refuse the poor city folk a ramble over our field, because, forsooth, they have not the advantage of our acquaintance?"

"How I abhor such things," said Bess; "the arrogant symbols of power."

"They disgrace human nature," said I.

"They shame the generous landscape," she said, "and they are abominable."

"Piggish!" quoth I, hotly. "Down with them!"

We looked forward to the coming of the poppies, did Bess and I, looked forward as only creatures of the city may look who have been long denied. I have forgotten to mention the existence of a house above the poppy field, a squat and wandering bungalow in which we had elected to forsake town traditions and live in fresher and more vigorous ways. The first poppies came, orange-yellow and golden in the standing grain, and we went about gleefully, as though drunken with their wine, and told each other that the poppies were there. We laughed at unexpected moments, in the midst of silences, and at times grew ashamed and stole forth secretly to gaze upon our treasury. But when the great wave of poppy-flame finally spilled itself down the field, we shouted aloud, and danced, and clapped our hands, freely and frankly mad.

And then came the Goths. My face was in a lather, the time of the first invasion, and I suspended my razor in mid-air to gaze out on my beloved field. At the far end I saw a little girl and a little boy, their arms filled with yellow spoil. Ah, thought I, an unwonted benevolence burgeoning, what a delight to me is their delight! It is sweet that children should pick poppies in my field. All summer shall they pick poppies in my field. But they must be little children, I added as an afterthought, and they must pick from the lower end—this last prompted by a glance at the great golden fellows nodding in the wheat beneath my window. Then the razor descended. Shaving was always an absorbing task, and I did not glance out of the window again until the operation was completed. And then I was bewildered. Surely this was not my poppy field. No—and yes, for there were the tall pines clustering austerely together on one side, the magnolia tree burdened with bloom, and the Japanese quinces splashing the driveway hedge with blood. Yes, it was the field, but no wave of poppy-flame spilled down it, nor did the great golden fellows nod in the wheat beneath my window. I rushed into a jacket and out of the house. In the far distance were disappearing two huge balls of colour, orange and yellow, for all the world like perambulating poppies of cyclopean breed.

"Johnny," said I to the nine-year-old son of my sister, "Johnny, whenever little girls come into our field to pick poppies, you must go down to them, and in a very quiet and gentlemanly manner, tell them it is not allowed."

Warm days came, and the sun drew another blaze from the free-bosomed earth. Whereupon a neighbour's little girl, at the behest of her mother, duly craved and received permission from Bess to gather a few poppies for decorative purposes. But of this I was uninformed, and when I descried her in the midst of the field I waved my arms like a semaphore against the sky.

"Little girl!" called I. "Little girl!"

The little girl's legs blurred the landscape as she fled, and in high elation I sought Bess to tell of the potency of my voice. Nobly she came to the rescue, departing forthwith on an expedition of conciliation and explanation to the little girl's mother. But to this day the little girl seeks cover at sight of me, and I know the mother will never be as cordial as she would otherwise have been.

Came dark, overcast days, stiff, driving winds, and pelting rains, day on day, without end, and the city folk cowered in their dwelling-places like flood-beset rats; and like rats, half-drowned and gasping, when the weather cleared they crawled out and up the green Piedmont slopes to bask in the blessed sunshine. And they invaded my field in swarms and droves, crushing the sweet wheat into the earth and with lustful hands ripping the poppies out by the roots.

"I shall put up the warnings against trespassing," I said.

"Yes," said Bess, with a sigh. "I'm afraid it is necessary."

The day was yet young when she sighed again:

"I'm afraid, O Man, that your signs are of no avail. People have forgotten how to read, these days."

I went out on the porch. A city nymph, in cool summer gown and picture hat, paused before one of my newly reared warnings and read it through with care. Profound deliberation characterized her movements. She was statuesquely tall, but with a toss of the head and a flirt of the skirt she dropped on hands and knees, crawled under the fence, and came to her feet on the inside with poppies in both her hands. I walked down the drive and talked ethically to her, and she went away. Then I put up more signs.

At one time, years ago, these hills were carpeted with poppies. As between the destructive forces and the will "to live," the poppies maintained an equilibrium with their environment. But the city folk constituted a new and terrible destructive force, the equilibrium was overthrown, and the poppies wellnigh perished. Since the city folk plucked those with the longest stems and biggest bowls, and since it is the law of kind to procreate kind, the long-stemmed, big-bowled poppies failed to go to seed, and a stunted, short-stemmed variety remained to the hills. And not only was it stunted and short-stemmed, but sparsely distributed as well. Each day and every day, for years and years, the city folk swarmed over the Piedmont Hills, and only here and there did the genius of the race survive in the form of miserable little flowers, close-clinging and quick-blooming, like children of the slums dragged hastily and precariously through youth to a shrivelled and futile maturity.

On the other hand, the poppies had prospered in my field; and not only had they been sheltered from the barbarians, but also from the birds. Long ago the field was sown in wheat, which went to seed unharvested each year, and in the cool depths of which the poppy seeds were hidden from the keen-eyed songsters. And further, climbing after the sun through the wheat stalks, the poppies grew taller and taller and more royal even than the primordial ones of the open.

So the city folk, gazing from the bare hills to my blazing, burning field, were sorely tempted, and, it must be told, as sorely fell. But no sorer was their fall than that of my beloved poppies. Where the grain holds the dew and takes the bite from the sun the soil is moist, and in such soil it is easier to pull the poppies out by the roots than to break the stalk. Now the city folk, like other folk, are inclined to move along the line of least resistance, and for each flower they gathered, there were also gathered many crisp-rolled buds and with them all the possibilities and future beauties of the plant for all time to come.

One of the city folk, a middle-aged gentleman, with white hands and shifty eyes, especially made life interesting for me. We called him the "Repeater," what of his ways. When from the porch we implored him to desist, he was wont slowly and casually to direct his steps toward the fence, simulating finely the actions of a man who had not heard, but whose walk, instead, had terminated of itself or of his own volition. To heighten this effect, now and again, still casually and carelessly, he would stoop and pluck another poppy. Thus did he deceitfully save himself the indignity of being put out, and rob us of the satisfaction of putting him out, but he came, and he came often, each time getting away with an able-bodied man's share of plunder.

It is not good to be of the city folk. Of this I am convinced. There is something in the mode of life that breeds an alarming condition of blindness and deafness, or so it seems with the city folk that come to my poppy field. Of the many to whom I have talked ethically not one has been found who ever saw the warnings so conspicuously displayed, while of those called out to from the porch, possibly one in fifty has heard. Also, I have discovered that the relation of city folk to country flowers is quite analogous to that of a starving man to food. No more than the starving man realizes that five pounds of meat is not so good as an ounce, do they realize that five hundred poppies crushed and bunched are less beautiful than two or three in a free cluster, where the green leaves and golden bowls may expand to their full loveliness.

Less forgivable than the unaesthetic are the mercenary. Hordes of young rascals plunder me and rob the future that they may stand on street corners and retail "California poppies, only five cents a bunch!" In spite of my precautions some of them made a dollar a day out of my field. One horde do I remember with keen regret. Reconnoitring for a possible dog, they applied at the kitchen door for "a drink of water, please." While they drank they were besought not to pick any flowers. They nodded, wiped their mouths, and proceeded to take themselves off by the side of the bungalow. They smote the poppy field beneath my windows, spread out fan-shaped six wide, picking with both hands, and ripped a swath of destruction through the very heart of the field. No cyclone travelled faster or destroyed more completely. I shouted after them, but they sped on the wings of the wind, great regal poppies, broken-stalked and mangled, trailing after them or cluttering their wake—the most high-handed act of piracy, I am confident, ever committed off the high seas.

One day I went a-fishing, and on that day a woman entered the field. Appeals and remonstrances from the porch having no effect upon her, Bess despatched a little girl to beg of her to pick no more poppies. The woman calmly went on picking. Then Bess herself went down through the heat of the day. But the woman went on picking, and while she picked she discussed property and proprietary rights, denying Bess's sovereignty until deeds and documents should be produced in proof thereof. And all the time she went on picking, never once overlooking her hand. She was a large woman, belligerent of aspect, and Bess was only a woman and not prone to fisticuffs. So the invader picked until she could pick no more, said "Good-day," and sailed majestically away.

"People have really grown worse in the last several years, I think," said Bess to me in a tired sort of voice that night, as we sat in the library after dinner.

Next day I was inclined to agree with her. "There's a woman and a little girl heading straight for the poppies," said May, a maid about the bungalow. I went out on the porch and waited their advent. They plunged through the pine trees and into the fields, and as the roots of the first poppies were pulled I called to them. They were about a hundred feet away. The woman and the little girl turned to the sound of my voice and looked at me. "Please do not pick the poppies," I pleaded. They pondered this for a minute; then the woman said something in an undertone to the little girl, and both backs jack-knifed as the slaughter recommenced. I shouted, but they had become suddenly deaf. I screamed, and so fiercely that the little girl wavered dubiously. And while the woman went on picking I could hear her in low tones heartening the little girl.

I recollected a siren whistle with which I was wont to summon Johnny, the son of my sister. It was a fearsome thing, of a kind to wake the dead, and I blew and blew, but the jack-knifed backs never unclasped. I do not mind with men, but I have never particularly favoured physical encounters with women; yet this woman, who encouraged a little girl in iniquity, tempted me.

I went into the bungalow and fetched my rifle. Flourishing it in a sanguinary manner and scowling fearsomely, I charged upon the invaders. The little girl fled, screaming, to the shelter of the pines, but the woman calmly went on picking. She took not the least notice. I had expected her to run at sight of me, and it was embarrassing. There was I, charging down the field like a wild bull upon a woman who would not get out of the way. I could only slow down, supremely conscious of how ridiculous it all was. At a distance of ten feet she straightened up and deigned to look at me. I came to a halt and blushed to the roots of my hair. Perhaps I really did frighten her (I sometimes try to persuade myself that this is so), or perhaps she took pity on me; but, at any rate, she stalked out of my field with great composure, nay, majesty, her arms brimming with orange and gold.

Nevertheless, thenceforward I saved my lungs and flourished my rifle. Also, I made fresh generalizations. To commit robbery women take advantage of their sex. Men have more respect for property than women. Men are less insistent in crime than women. And women are less afraid of guns than men. Likewise, we conquer the earth in hazard and battle by the virtues of our mothers. We are a race of land-robbers and sea-robbers, we Anglo-Saxons, and small wonder, when we suckle at the breasts of a breed of women such as maraud my poppy field.

Still the pillage went on. Sirens and gun-flourishings were without avail. The city folk were great of heart and undismayed, and I noted the habit of "repeating" was becoming general. What booted it how often they were driven forth if each time they were permitted to carry away their ill-gotten plunder? When one has turned the same person away twice and thrice an emotion arises somewhat akin to homicide. And when one has once become conscious of this sanguinary feeling his whole destiny seems to grip hold of him and drag him into the abyss. More than once I found myself unconsciously pulling the rifle into position to get a sight on the miserable trespassers. In my sleep I slew them in manifold ways and threw their carcasses into the reservoir. Each day the temptation to shoot them in the legs became more luring, and every day I felt my fate calling to me imperiously. Visions of the gallows rose up before me, and with the hemp about my neck I saw stretched out the pitiless future of my children, dark with disgrace and shame. I became afraid of myself, and Bess went about with anxious face, privily beseeching my friends to entice me into taking a vacation. Then, and at the last gasp, came the thought that saved me: WHY NOT CONFIS-CATE? If their forays were bootless, in the nature of things their forays would cease.

The first to enter my field thereafter was a man.

I was waiting for him And, oh joy! it was the "Repeater" himself, smugly complacent with knowledge of past success. I dropped the rifle negligently across the hollow of my arm and went down to him.

"I am sorry to trouble you for those poppies," I said in my oiliest tones; "but really, you know, I must have them."

He regarded me speechlessly. It must have made a great picture. It surely was dramatic. With the rifle across my arm and my suave request still ringing in my ears, I felt like Black Bart, and Jesse James, and Jack Sheppard, and Robin Hood, and whole generations of highwaymen.

"Come, come," I said, a little sharply and in what I imagined was the true fashion; "I am sorry to inconvenience you, believe me, but I must have those poppies."

I absently shifted the gun and smiled. That fetched him. Without a word he passed them over and turned his toes toward the fence, but no longer casual and careless was his carriage, I nor did he stoop to pick the occasional poppy by the way. That was the last of the "Repeater." I could see by his eyes that he did not like me, and his back reproached me all the way down the field and out of sight.

From that day the bungalow has been flooded with poppies. Every vase and earthen jar is filled with them. They blaze on every mantel and run riot through all the rooms. I present them to my friends in huge bunches, and still the kind city folk come and gather more for me. "Sit down for a moment," I say to the departing guest. And there we sit in the shade of the porch while aspiring city creatures pluck my poppies and sweat under the brazen sun. And when their arms are sufficiently weighted with my yellow glories, I go down with the rifle over my arm and disburden them. Thus have I become convinced that every situation has its compensations.

Confiscation was successful, so far as it went; but I had forgotten one thing; namely, the vast number of the city folk. Though the old transgressors came no more, new ones arrived every day, and I found myself confronted with the titanic task of educating a whole cityful to the inexpediency of raiding my poppy field. During the process of disburdening them I was accustomed to explaining my side of the case, but I soon gave this over. It was a waste of breath. They could not understand. To one lady, who insinuated that I was miserly, I said:

"My dear madam, no hardship is worked upon you. Had I not been parsimonious yesterday and the day before, these poppies would have been picked by the city hordes of that day and the day before, and your eyes, which to-day have discovered this field, would have beheld no poppies at all. The poppies you may not pick to-day are the poppies I did not permit to be picked yesterday and the day before. Therefore, believe me, you are denied nothing."

"But the poppies are here to-day," she said, glaring carnivorously upon their glow and splendour.

"I will pay you for them," said a gentleman, at another time. (I had just relieved him of an armful.) I felt a sudden shame, I know not why, unless it be that his words had just made clear to me that a monetary as well as an aesthetic value was attached to my flowers. The apparent sordidness of my position overwhelmed me, and I said weakly: "I do not sell my poppies. You may have what you have picked." But before the week was out I confronted the same gentleman again. "I will pay you for them," he said. "Yes," I said, "you may pay me for them. Twenty dollars, please." He gasped, looked at me searchingly, gasped again, and silently and sadly put the poppies down. But it remained, as usual, for a woman to attain the sheerest pitch of audacity. When I declined payment and demanded my plucked beauties, she refused to give them up. "I picked these poppies," she said, "and my time is worth money. When you have paid me for my time you may have them." Her cheeks flamed rebellion, and her face, withal a pretty one, was set and determined. Now, I was a man of the hill tribes, and she a mere woman of the city folk, and though it is not my inclination to enter into details, it is my pleasure to state that that bunch of poppies subsequently glorified the bungalow and that the woman departed to the city unpaid. Anyway, they were my poppies.

"They are God's poppies," said the Radiant Young Radical, democratically shocked at sight of me turning city folk out of my field. And for two weeks she hated me with a deathless hatred. I sought her out and explained. I explained at length. I told the story of the poppy as Maeterlinck has told the life of the bee. I treated the question biologically, psychologically, and sociologically, I discussed it ethically and aesthetically. I grew warm over it, and impassioned; and when I had done, she professed conversion, but in my heart of hearts I knew it to be compassion. I fled to other friends for consolation. I retold the story of the poppy. They did not appear supremely interested. I grew excited. They were surprised and pained. They looked at me curiously. "It ill-befits your dignity to squabble over poppies," they said. "It is unbecoming."

I fled away to yet other friends. I sought vindication. The thing had become vital, and I needs must put myself right. I felt called upon to explain, though well knowing that he who explains is lost. I told the story of the poppy over again. I went into the minutest details. I added to it, and expanded. I talked myself hoarse, and when I could talk no more they looked bored. Also, they said insipid things, and soothful things, and things concerning other things, and not at all to the point. I was consumed with anger, and there and then I renounced them all.

At the bungalow I lie in wait for chance visitors. Craftily I broach the subject, watching their faces closely the while to detect first signs of disapprobation, whereupon I empty long-stored vials of wrath upon their heads. I wrangle for hours with whosoever does not say I am right. I am become like Guy de Maupassant's old man who picked up a piece of string. I am incessantly explaining, and nobody will understand. I have become more brusque in my treatment of the predatory city folk. No longer do I take delight in their disburdenment, for it has become an onerous duty, a wearisome and distasteful task. My friends look askance and murmur pityingly on the side when we meet in the city. They rarely come to see me now. They are afraid. I am an embittered and disappointed man, and all the light seems to have gone out of my life and into my blazing field. So one pays for things.

PIEDMONT, CALIFORNIA., April 1902.

Jack London

THE SHRINKAGE OF THE PLANET

What a tremendous affair it was, the world of Homer, with its indeterminate boundaries, vast regions, and immeasurable distances. The Mediterranean and the Euxine were illimitable stretches of ocean waste over which years could be spent in endless wandering. On their mysterious shores were the improbable homes of impossible peoples. The Great Sea, the Broad Sea, the Boundless Sea; the Ethiopians, "dwelling far away, the most distant of men," and the Cimmerians, "covered with darkness and cloud," where "baleful night is spread over timid mortals." Phonicia was a sore journey, Egypt simply unattainable, while the Pillars of Hercules marked the extreme edge of the universe. Ulysses was nine days in sailing from Ismarus the city of the Ciconians, to the country of the Lotus-eaters—a period of time which to-day would breed anxiety in the hearts of the underwriters should it be occupied by the slowest tramp steamer in traversing the Mediterranean and Black Seas from Gibraltar to Sebastopol.

Homer's world, restricted to less than a drummer's circuit, was nevertheless immense, surrounded by a thin veneer of universe—the Stream of Ocean. But how it has shrunk! To-day, precisely charted, weighed, and measured, a thousand times larger than the world of Homer, it is become a tiny speck, gyrating to immutable law through a universe the bounds of which have been pushed incalculably back. The light of Algol shines upon it—a light which travels at one hundred and ninety thousand miles per second, yet requires forty-seven years to reach its destination. And the denizens of this puny ball have come to know that Algol possesses an invisible companion, three and a quarter millions of miles away, and that the twain move in their respective orbits at rates of fifty-five and twenty-six miles per second. They also know that beyond it are great chasms of space, innumerable worlds, and vast star systems.

While much of the shrinkage to which the planet has been subjected is due to the increased knowledge of mathematics and physics, an equal, if not greater, portion may be ascribed to the perfection of the means of locomotion and communication. The enlargement of stellar space, demonstrating with stunning force the insignificance of the earth, has been negative in its effect; but the quickening of travel and intercourse, by making the earth's parts accessible and knitting them together, has been positive.

The advantage of the animal over the vegetable kingdom is obvious. The cabbage, should its environment tend to become worse, must live it out, or die; the rabbit may move on in quest of a better. But, after all, the swift-footed creatures are circumscribed in their wanderings. The first large river almost inevitably bars their way, and certainly the first salt sea becomes an impassable obstacle. Better locomotion may be classed as one of the prime aims of the old natural selection; for in that primordial day the race was to the swift as surely as the battle to the strong. But man, already pre-eminent in the common domain because of other faculties, was not content with the one form of locomotion afforded by his lower limbs. He swam in the sea, and, still better, becoming aware of the buoyant virtues of wood, learned to navigate its surface. Likewise, from among the land animals he chose the more likely to bear him and his burdens. The next step was the domestication of these useful aids. Here, in its organic significance, natural selection ceased to concern itself with locomotion. Man had displayed his impatience at her tedious methods and his own superiority in the hastening of affairs. Thenceforth he must depend upon himself, and faster-swimming or faster-running men ceased to be bred. The one, half-amphibian, breasting the water with muscular arms, could not hope to overtake or escape an enemy who propelled a fire-hollowed tree trunk by means of a wooden paddle; nor could the other, trusting to his own nimbleness, compete with a foe who careered wildly across the plain on the back of a half-broken stallion.

So, in that dim day, man took upon himself the task of increasing his dominion over space and time, and right nobly has he acquitted himself. Because of it he became a road builder and a bridge builder; likewise, he wove clumsy sails of rush and matting. At a very remote period he must also have recognized that force moves along the line of least resistance, and in virtue thereof, placed upon his craft rude keels which enabled him to beat to windward in a seaway. As he excelled in these humble arts, just so did he add to his power over his less progressive fellows and lay the foundations for the first glimmering civilizations—crude they were beyond conception, sporadic and ephemeral, but each formed a necessary part of the groundwork upon which was to rise the mighty civilization of our latter-day world.

Divorced from the general history of man's upward climb, it would seem incredible that so long a time should elapse between the moment of his first improvements over nature in the matter of locomotion and that of the radical changes he was ultimately to compass. The principles which were his before history was, were his, neither more nor less, even to the present century. He utilized improved applications, but the principles of themselves were ever the same, whether in the war chariots of Achilles and Pharaoh or the mail-coach and diligence of the European traveller, the cavalry of the Huns or of Prince Rupert, the triremes and galleys of Greece and Rome or the East India-men and clipper ships of the last century. But when the moment came to alter the methods of travel, the change was so sweeping that it may be safely classed as a revolution. Though the discovery of steam attaches to the honour of the last century, the potency of the new power was not felt till the beginning of this. By 1800 small steamers were being used for coasting purposes in England; 1830 witnessed the opening of the Liverpool and Manchester Railway; while it was not until 1838 that the Atlantic was first crossed by the steamships Great Western and Sirius. In 1869 the East was made next-door neighbour to the West. Over almost the same ground where had toiled the caravans of a thousand generations, the Suez Canal was dug. Clive, during his first trip, was a year and a half en route from England to India; were he alive to-day he could journey to Calcutta in twenty-two days. After reading De Quincey's hyperbolical description of the English mail-coach, one cannot down the desire to place that remarkable man on the pilot of the White Mail or of the Twentieth Century.

But this tremendous change in the means of locomotion meant far more than the mere rapid transit of men from place to place. Until then, though its influence and worth cannot be overestimated, commerce had eked out a precarious and costly existence. The fortuitous played too large a part in the trade of men. The mischances by land and sea, the mistakes and delays, were adverse elements of no mean proportions. But improved locomotion meant improved carrying, and commerce received an impetus as remarkable as it was unexpected. In his fondest fancies James Watt could not have foreseen even the approximate result of his invention, the Hercules which was to spring from the puny child of his brain and hands. An illuminating spectacle, were it possible, would be afforded by summoning him from among the Shades to a place in the engine-room of an ocean greyhound. The humblest trimmer would treat him with the indulgence of a child; while an oiler, a greasy nimbus about his head and in his hand, as sceptre, a long-snouted can, would indeed appear to him a demigod and ruler of forces beyond his ken.

It has ever been the world's dictum that empire and commerce go hand in hand. In the past the one was impossible without the other. Rome gathered to herself the wealth of the Mediterranean nations, and it was only by an unwise distribution of it that she became emasculated and lost both power and trade. With a just system of economics it is highly probable that for centuries she could have held back the welling tide of the Germanic peoples. When upon her ruins rose the institutions of the conquering Teutons, commerce slipped away, and with it empire. In the present, empire and commerce have become interdependent. Such wonders has the industrial revolution wrought in a few swift decades, and so great has been the shrinkage of the planet, that the industrial nations have long since felt the imperative demand for foreign markets. The favoured portions of the earth are occupied. From their seats in the temperate zones the militant commercial nations proceed to the exploitation of the tropics, and for the possession of these they rush to war hot-footed. Like wolves at the end of a gorge, they wrangle over the fragments. There are no more planets, no more fragments, and they are yet hungry. There are no longer Cimmerians and Ethiopians, in wide-stretching lands, awaiting them. On either hand they confront the naked poles, and they recoil from unnavigable space to an intenser struggle among themselves. And all the while the planet shrinks beneath their grasp.

Of this struggle one thing may be safely predicated; a commercial power must be a sea power. Upon the control of the sea depends the control of trade. Carthage threatened Rome till she lost her navy; and then for thirteen days the smoke of her burning rose to the skies, and the ground was ploughed and sown with salt on the site of her most splendid edifices. The cities of Italy were the world's merchants till new trade routes were discovered and the dominion of the sea passed on to the west and fell into other hands. Spain and Portugal, inaugurating an era of maritime discovery, divided the new world between them, but gave way before a breed of sea-rovers, who, after many generations of attachment to the soil, had returned to their ancient element. With the destruction of her Armada Spain's colossal dream of colonial empire passed away. Against the new power Holland strove in vain, and when France acknowledged the superiority of the Briton upon the sea, she at the same time relinquished her designs upon the world. Hampered by her feeble navy, her contest for supremacy upon the land was her last effort and with the passing of Napoleon she retired within herself to struggle with herself as best she might. For fifty years England held undisputed sway upon the sea, controlled markets, and domineered trade, laying, during that period, the foundations of her empire. Since then other naval powers have arisen, their attitudes bearing significantly upon the future; for they have learned that the mastery of the world belongs to the masters of the sea.

That many of the phases of this world shrinkage are pathetic, goes without question. There is much to condemn in the rise of the economic over the imaginative spirit, much for which the energetic Philistine can never atone. Perhaps the deepest pathos of all may be found in the spectacle of John Ruskin weeping at the profanation of the world by the vandalism of the age. Steam launches violate the sanctity of the Venetian canals; where Xerxes bridged the Hellespont ply the filthy funnels of our modern shipping; electric cars run in the shadow of the pyramids; and it was only the other day that Lord Kitchener was in a railroad wreck near the site of ancient Luxor. But there is always the other side. If the economic man has defiled temples and despoiled nature, he has also preserved. He has policed the world and parked it, reduced the dangers of life and limb, made the tenure of existence less precarious, and rendered a general relapse of society impossible. There can never again be an intellectual holocaust, such as the burning of the Alexandrian library. Civilizations may wax and wane, but the totality of knowledge cannot decrease. With the possible exception of a few trade secrets, arts and sciences may be discarded, but they can never be lost. And these things must remain true until the end of man's time upon the earth.

Up to yesterday communication for any distance beyond the sound of the human voice or the sight of the human eye was bound up with locomotion. A letter presupposed a carrier. The messenger started with the message, and he could not but avail himself of the prevailing modes of travel. If the voyage to Australia required four months, four months were required for communication; by no known means could this time be lessened. But with the advent of the telegraph and telephone, communication and locomotion were divorced. In a few hours, at most, there could be performed what by the old way would have required months. In 1837 the needle telegraph was invented, and nine years later the Electric Telegraph Company was formed for the purpose of bringing it into general use. Government postal systems also came into being, later to consolidate into an international union and to group the nations of the earth into a local neighbourhood. The effects of all this are obvious, and no fitter illustration may be presented than the fact that to-day, in the matter of communication, the Klondike is virtually nearer to Boston than was Bunker Hill in the time of Warren.

A contemporaneous and remarkable shrinkage of a vast stretch of territory may be instanced in the Northland. From its rise at Lake Linderman the Yukon runs twenty-five hundred miles to Bering Sea, traversing an almost unknown region, the remote recesses of which had never felt the moccasined foot of the pathfinder. At occasional intervals men wallowed into its dismal fastnesses, or emerged gaunt and famine-worn. But in the fall of 1896 a great gold strike was made—greater than any since the days of California and Australia; yet, so rude were the means of communication, nearly a year elapsed before the news of it reached the eager ear of the world. Passionate pilgrims disembarked their outfits at Dyea. Over the terrible Chilcoot Pass the trail led to the lakes, thirty miles away. Carriage was yet in its most primitive stage, the road builder and bridge builder unheard of. With heavy packs upon their backs men plunged waist-deep into hideous quagmires, bridged mountain torrents by felling trees across them, toiled against the precipitous slopes of the ice-worn mountains, and crossed the dizzy faces of innumerable glaciers. When, after incalculable toil they reached the lakes, they went into the woods, sawed pine trees into lumber by hand, and built it into boats. In these, overloaded, unseaworthy, they battled down the long chain of lakes. Within the memory of the writer there lingers the picture of a sheltered nook on the shores of Lake Le

Barge, in which half a thousand gold seekers lay storm-bound. Day after day they struggled against the seas in the teeth of a northerly gale, and night after night returned to their camps, repulsed but not disheartened. At the rapids they ran their boats through, hit or miss, and after infinite toil and hardship, on the breast of a jarring ice flood, arrived at the Klondike. From the beach at Dyea to the eddy below the Barracks at Dawson, they had paid for their temerity the tax of human life demanded by the elements. A year later, so greatly had the country shrunk, the tourist, on disembarking from the ocean steamship, took his seat in a modern railway coach. A few hours later, at Lake Bennet, he stepped aboard a commodious river steamer. At the rapids he rode around on a tramway to take passage on another steamer below. And in a few hours more he was in Dawson, without having once soiled the lustre of his civilized foot-gear. Did he wish to communicate with the outside world, he strolled into the telegraph office. A few short months before he would have written a letter and deemed himself favoured above mortals were it delivered within the year.

From man's drawing the world closer and closer together, his own affairs and institutions have consolidated. Concentration may typify the chief movement of the age—concentration, classification, order; the reduction of friction between the parts of the social organism. The urban tendency of the rural populations led to terrible congestion in the great cities. There was stifling and impure air, and lo, rapid transit at once attacked the evil. Every great city has become but the nucleus of a greater city which surrounds it; the one the seat of business, the other the seat of domestic happiness. Between the two, night and morning, by electric road, steam railway, and bicycle path, ebbs and flows the middle-class population. And in the same direction lies the remedy for the tenement evil. In the cleansing country air the slum cannot exist. Improvement in road-beds and the means of locomotion, a tremor of altruism, a little legislation, and the city by day will sleep in the country by night.

What a play-ball has this planet of ours become! Steam has made its parts accessible and drawn them closer together. The telegraph annihilates space and time. Each morning every part knows what every other part is thinking, contemplating, or doing. A discovery in a German laboratory is being demonstrated in San Francisco within twenty-four hours. A book written in South Africa is published by simultaneous copyright in every English-speaking country, and on the following day is in the hands of the translators. The death of an obscure missionary in China, or of a whisky smuggler in the South Seas, is served up, the world over, with the morning toast. The wheat output of Argentine or the gold of Klondike is known wherever men meet and trade. Shrinkage or centralization has been such that the humblest clerk in any metropolis may place his hand on the pulse of the world. And because of all this, everywhere is growing order and organization. The church, the state; men, women, and children; the criminal and the law, the honest man and the thief, industry and commerce, capital and labour, the trades and the professions, the arts and the sciences—all are organizing for pleasure, profit, policy, or intellectual pursuit. They have come to know the strength of numbers, solidly phalanxed and driving onward with singleness of purpose. These purposes may be various and many, but one and all, ever discovering new mutual interests and objects, obeying a law which is beyond them, these petty aggregations draw closer together, forming greater aggregations and congeries of aggregations. And these, in turn, vaguely merging each into each, present glimmering adumbrations of the coming human solidarity which shall be man's crowning glory.

OAKLAND, CALIFORNIA., January 1900.

THE HOUSE BEAUTIFUL

Speaking of homes, I am building one now, and I venture to assert that very few homes have received more serious thought in the planning. Let me tell you about it. In the first place, there will be no grounds whatever, no fences, lawns, nor flowers. Roughly, the dimensions will be forty-five feet by fifteen. That is, it will be fifteen feet wide at its widest—and, if you will pardon the bull, it will be narrower than it is wide.

The details must submit to the general plan of economy. There will be no veranda, no porch entrances, no grand staircases. I'm ashamed to say how steep the stairways are going to be. The bedrooms will be seven by seven, and one will be even smaller. A bedroom is only good to sleep in, anyway. There will be no hallway, thank goodness. Rooms were made to go through. Why a separate passage for traffic?

The bath-room will be a trifle larger than the size of the smallest bath-tub—it won't require so much work to keep in order. The kitchen won't be very much larger, but this will make it easy for the cook. In place of a drawing-room, there will be a large living-room-fourteen by six. The walls of this room will be covered with books, and it can serve as library and smoking-room as well. Then, the floor-space not being occupied, we shall use the room as a dining-room. Incidentally, such a room not being used after bedtime, the cook and the second boy can sleep in it. One thing that I am temperamentally opposed to is waste, and why should all this splendid room be wasted at night when we do not occupy it?

Jack London

My ideas are cramped, you say?—Oh, I forgot to tell you that this home I am describing is to be a floating home, and that my wife and I are to journey around the world in it for the matter of seven years or more. I forgot also to state that there will be an engine-room in it for a seventy-horse-power engine, a dynamo, storage batteries, etc.; tanks for water to last long weeks at sea; space for fifteen hundred gallons of gasolene, fire extinguishers, and life-preservers; and a great store-room for food, spare sails, anchors, hawsers, tackles, and a thousand and one other things.

Since I have not yet built my land house, I haven't got beyond a few general ideas, and in presenting them I feel as cocksure as the unmarried woman who writes the column in the Sunday supplement on how to rear children. My first idea about a house is that it should be built to live in. Throughout the house, in all the building of it, this should be the paramount idea. It must be granted that this idea is lost sight of by countless persons who build houses apparently for every purpose under the sun except to live in them.

Perhaps it is because of the practical life I have lived that I worship utility and have come to believe that utility and beauty should be one, and that there is no utility that need not be beautiful. What finer beauty than strength—whether it be airy steel, or massive masonry, or a woman's hand? A plain black leather strap is beautiful. It is all strength and all utility, and it is beautiful. It efficiently performs work in the world, and it is good to look upon. Perhaps it is because it is useful that it is beautiful. I do not know. I sometimes wonder.

A boat on the sea is beautiful. Yet it is not built for beauty. Every graceful line of it is a utility, is designed to perform work. It is created for the express purpose of dividing the water in front of it, of gliding over the water beneath it, of leaving the water behind it—and all with the least possible wastage of stress and friction. It is not created for the purpose of filling the eye with beauty. It is created for the purpose of moving through the sea and over the sea with the smallest resistance and the greatest stability; yet, somehow, it does fill the eye with its beauty. And in so far as a boat fails in its purpose, by that much does it diminish in beauty.

I am still a long way from the house I have in my mind some day to build, yet I have arrived somewhere. I have discovered, to my own satisfaction at any rate, that beauty and utility should be one. In applying this general idea to the building of a house, it may be stated, in another and better way; namely, construction and decoration must be one. This idea is more important than the building of the house, for without the idea the house so built is certain to be an insult to intelligence and beauty-love.

I bought a house in a hurry in the city of Oakland some time ago. I do not live in it. I sleep in it half a dozen times a year. I do not love the house. I am hurt every time I look at it. No drunken rowdy or political enemy can insult me so deeply as that house does. Let me tell you why. It is an ordinary two-storey frame house. After it was built, the criminal that constructed it nailed on, at the corners perpendicularly, some two-inch fluted planks. These planks rise the height of the house, and to a drunken man have the appearance of fluted columns. To complete the illusion in the eyes of the drunken man, the planks are topped with wooden Ionic capitals, nailed on, and in, I may say, bas-relief.

When I analyze the irritation these fluted planks cause in me, I find the reason in the fact that the first rule for building a house has been violated. These decorative planks are no part of the construction. They have no use, no work to perform. They are plastered gawds that tell lies that nobody believes. A column is made for the purpose of supporting weight; this is its use. A column, when it is a utility, is beautiful. The fluted wooden columns nailed on outside my house are not utilities. They are not beautiful. They are nightmares. They not only support no weight, but they themselves are a weight that drags upon the supports of the house. Some day, when I get time, one of two things will surely happen. Either I'll go forth and murder the man who perpetrated the atrocity, or else I'll take an axe and chop off the lying, fluted planks.

A thing must be true, or it is not beautiful, any more than a painted wanton is beautiful, any more than a sky-scraper is beautiful that is intrinsically and structurally light and that has a false massiveness of pillars plastered on outside. The true sky-scraper IS beautiful—and this is the reluctant admission of a man who dislikes humanity-festering cities. The true sky-scraper is beautiful, and it is beautiful in so far as it is true. In its construction it is light and airy, therefore in its appearance it must be light and airy. It dare not, if it wishes to be beautiful, lay claim to what it is not. And it should not bulk on the city-scape like Leviathan; it should rise and soar, light and airy and fairylike.

Man is an ethical animal—or, at least, he is more ethical than any other animal. Wherefore he has certain yearnings for honesty. And in no way can these yearnings be more thoroughly satisfied than by the honesty of the house in which he lives and passes the greater part of his life.

They that dwelt in San Francisco were dishonest. They lied and cheated in their business life (like the dwellers in all cities), and because they lied and cheated in their business life, they lied and cheated in the buildings they erected. Upon the tops of the simple, severe walls of their buildings they plastered huge projecting cornices. These cornices were not part of the construction. They made believe to be part of the construction, and they were lies. The earth wrinkled its back for twenty-eight seconds, and the lying cornices crashed down as all lies are doomed to crash down. In this particular instance, the lies crashed down upon the heads of the people fleeing from their reeling habitations, and many were killed. They paid the penalty of dishonesty.

Not alone should the construction of a house be truthful and honest, but the material must be honest. They that lived in San Francisco were dishonest in the material they used. They sold one quality of material and delivered another quality of material. They always delivered an inferior quality. There is not one case recorded in the business history of San Francisco where a contractor or builder delivered a quality superior to the one sold. A seven-million-dollar city hall became thirty cents in twenty-eight seconds. Because the mortar was not honest, a thousand walls crashed down and scores of lives were snuffed out. There is something, after all, in the contention of a few religionists that the San Francisco earthquake was a punishment for sin. It was a punishment for sin; but it was not for sin against God. The people of San Francisco sinned against themselves.

An honest house tells the truth about itself. There is a house here in Glen Ellen. It stands on a corner. It is built of beautiful red stone. Yet it is not beautiful. On three sides the stone is joined and pointed. The fourth side is the rear. It faces the back yard. The stone is not pointed. It is all a smudge of dirty mortar, with here and there bricks worked in when the stone gave out. The house is not what it seems. It is a lie. All three of the walls spend their time lying about the fourth wall. They keep shouting out that the fourth wall is as beautiful as they. If I lived long in that house I should not be responsible for my morals. The house is like a man in purple and fine linen, who hasn't had a bath for a month. If I lived long in that house I should become a dandy and cut out bathing—for the same reason, I suppose, that an African is black and that an Eskimo eats whale-blubber. I shall not build a house like that house.

Last year I started to build a barn. A man who was a liar undertook to do the stonework and concrete work for me. He could not tell the truth to my face; he could not tell the truth in his work. I was building for posterity. The concrete foundations were four feet wide and sunk three and one-half feet into the earth. The stone walls were two feet thick and nine feet high. Upon them were to rest the great beams that were to carry all the weight of hay and the forty tons of the roof. The man who was a liar made beautiful stone walls. I used to stand alongside of them and love them. I caressed their massive strength with my hands. I thought about them in bed, before I went to sheep. And they were lies.

Came the earthquake. Fortunately the rest of the building of the barn had been postponed. The beautiful stone walls cracked in all directions. I started, to repair, and discovered the whole enormous lie. The walls were shells. On each face were beautiful, massive stones—on edge. The inside was hollow. This hollow in some places was filled with clay and loose gravel. In other places it was filled with air and emptiness, with here and there a piece of kindling-wood or dry-goods box, to aid in the making of the shell. The walls were lies. They were beautiful, but they were not useful. Construction and decoration had been divorced. The walls were all decoration. They hadn't any construction in them. "As God lets Satan live," I let that lying man live, but—I have built new walls from the foundation up.

And now to my own house beautiful, which I shall build some seven or ten years from now. I have a few general ideas about it. It must be honest in construction, material, and appearance. If any feature of it, despite my efforts, shall tell lies, I shall remove that feature. Utility and beauty must be indissolubly wedded. Construction and decoration must be one. If the particular details keep true to these general ideas, all will be well.

I have not thought of many details. But here are a few. Take the bath-room, for instance. It shall be as beautiful as any room in the house, just as it will be as useful. The chance is, that it will be the most expensive room in the house. Upon that we are resolved—even if we are compelled to build it first, and to live in a tent till we can get more money to go on with the rest of the house. In the bath-room no delights of the bath shall be lacking. Also, a large part of the expensiveness will be due to the use of material that will make it easy to keep the bathroom clean and in order. Why should a servant toil unduly that my body may be clean? On the other hand, the honesty of my own flesh, and the square dealing I give it, are more important than all the admiration of my friends for expensive decorative schemes and magnificent trivialities. More delightful to me is a body that sings than a stately and costly grand staircase built for show. Not that I like grand staircases less, but that I like bath-rooms more.

I often regret that I was born in this particular period of the world. In the matter of servants, how I wish I were living in the golden future of the world, where there will be no servants —naught but service of love. But in the meantime, living here and now, being practical, understanding the rationality and the necessity of the division of labour, I accept servants. But such acceptance does not justify me in lack of consideration for them. In my house beautiful their rooms shall not be dens and holes. And on this score I foresee a fight with the architect. They shall have bath-rooms, toilet conveniences, and comforts for their leisure time and human life—if I have to work Sundays to pay for it. Even under the division of labour I recognize that no man has a right to servants who will not treat them as humans compounded of the same clay as himself, with similar bundles of nerves and desires, contradictions, irritabilities, and lovablenesses. Heaven in the drawing-room and hell in the kitchen is not the atmosphere for a growing child to breathe—nor an adult either. One of the great and selfish objections to chattel slavery was the effect on the masters themselves.

And because of the foregoing, one chief aim in the building of my house beautiful will be to have a house that will require the minimum of trouble and work to keep clean and orderly. It will be no spick and span and polished house, with an immaculateness that testifies to the tragedy of drudge. I live in California where the days are warm. I'd prefer that the servants had three hours to go swimming (or hammocking) than be compelled to spend those three hours in keeping the house spick and span. Therefore it devolves upon me to build a house that can be kept clean and orderly without the need of those three hours.

But underneath the spick and span there is something more

dreadful than the servitude of the servants. This dreadful thing is the philosophy of the spick and span. In Korea the national costume is white. Nobleman and coolie dress alike in white. It is hell on the women who do the washing, but there is more in it than that. The coolie cannot keep his white clothes clean. He toils and they get dirty. The dirty white of his costume is the token of his inferiority. The nobleman's dress is always spotless white. It means that he doesn't have to work. But it means, further, that somebody else has to work for him. His superiority is not based upon song-craft nor state-craft, upon the foot-races he has run nor the wrestlers he has thrown. His superiority is based upon the fact that he doesn't have to work, and that others are compelled to work for him. And so the Korean drone flaunts his clean white clothes, for the same reason that the Chinese flaunts his monstrous finger-nails, and the white man and woman flaunt the spick-and-spanness of their spotless houses.

There will be hardwood floors in my house beautiful. But these floors will not be polished mirrors nor skating-rinks. They will be just plain and common hardwood floors. Beautiful carpets are not beautiful to the mind that knows they are filled with germs and bacilli. They are no more beautiful than the hectic flush of fever, or the silvery skin of leprosy. Besides, carpets enslave. A thing that enslaves is a monster, and monsters are not beautiful.

The fireplaces in my house will be many and large. Small fires and cold weather mean hermetically-sealed rooms and a jealous cherishing of heated and filth-laden air. With large fire-places and generous heat, some windows may be open all the time, and without hardship all the windows can be opened every little while and the rooms flushed with clean pure air. I have nearly died in the stagnant, rotten air of other people's houses—especially in the Eastern states. In Maine I have slept in a room with storm-windows immovable, and with one small pane five inches by six, that could be opened. Did I say slept? I panted with my mouth in the opening and blasphemed till I ruined all my chances of heaven.

For countless thousands of years my ancestors have lived and died and drawn all their breaths in the open air. It is only recently that we have begun to live in houses. The change is a hardship, especially on the lungs. I've got only one pair of lungs, and I haven't the address of any repair-shop. Wherefore I stick by the open air as much as possible. For this reason my house will have large verandas, and, near to the kitchen, there will be a veranda dining-room. Also, there will be a veranda fireplace, where we can breathe fresh air and be comfortable when the evenings are touched with frost.

I have a plan for my own bedroom. I spend long hours in bed, reading, studying, and working. I have tried sleeping in the open, but the lamp attracts all the creeping, crawling, butting, flying, fluttering things to the pages of my book, into my ears and blankets, and down the back of my neck. So my bedroom shall be indoors.

But it will be, not be of, indoors. Three sides of it will be open. The fourth side will divide it from the rest of the house. The three sides will be screened against the creeping, fluttering things, but not against the good fresh air and all the breezes that blow. For protection against storm, to keep out the driving rain, there will be a sliding glass, so made that when not in use it will occupy small space and shut out very little air.

There is little more to say about this house. I am to build seven or ten years from now. There is plenty of time in which to work up all the details in accord with the general principles I have laid down. It will be a usable house and a beautiful house, wherein the aesthetic guest can find comfort for his eyes as well as for his body. It will be a happy house—or else I'll burn it down. It will be a house of air and sunshine and laughter. These three cannot be divorced. Laughter without air and sunshine becomes morbid, decadent, demoniac. I have in me a thousand generations. Laughter that is decadent is not good for these thousand generations.

GLEN ELLEN, CALIFORNIA., July 1906.

Jack London

THE GOLD HUNTERS OF THE NORTH

"Where the Northern Lights come down a' nights to dance on the houseless snow."

"Ivan, I forbid you to go farther in this undertaking. Not a word about this, or we are all undone. Let the Americans and the English know that we have gold in these mountains, then we are ruined. They will rush in on us by thousands, and crowd us to the wall—to the death."

So spoke the old Russian governor, Baranov, at Sitka, in 1804, to one of his Slavonian hunters, who had just drawn from his pocket a handful of golden nuggets. Full well Baranov, fur trader and autocrat, understood and feared the coming of the sturdy, indomitable gold hunters of Anglo-Saxon stock. And thus he suppressed the news, as did the governors that followed him, so that when the United States bought Alaska in 1867, she bought it for its furs and fisheries, without a thought of its treasures underground.

No sooner, however, had Alaska become American soil than thousands of our adventurers were afoot and afloat for the north. They were the men of "the days of gold," the men of California, Fraser, Cassiar, and Cariboo. With the mysterious, infinite faith of the prospector, they believed that the gold streak, which ran through the Americas from Cape Horn to California, did not "peter out" in British Columbia. That it extended farther north, was their creed, and "Farther North" became their cry. No time was lost, and in the early seventies, leaving the Treadwell and the Silver Bow Basin to be discovered by those who came after, they went plunging on into the white unknown. North, farther north, they struggled, till their picks rang in the frozen beaches of the Arctic Ocean, and they shivered by driftwood fires on the ruby sands of Nome.

But first, in order that this colossal adventure may be fully grasped, the recentness and the remoteness of Alaska must be emphasized. The interior of Alaska and the contiguous Canadian territory was a vast wilderness. Its hundreds of thousands of square miles were as dark and chartless as Darkest Africa. In 1847, when the first Hudson Bay Company agents crossed over the Rockies from the Mackenzie to poach on the preserves of the Russian Bear, they thought that the Yukon flowed north and emptied into the Arctic Ocean. Hundreds of miles below, however, were the outposts of the Russian traders. They, in turn, did not know where the Yukon had its source, and it was not till later that Russ and Saxon learned that it was the same mighty stream they were occupying. And a little over ten years later, Frederick Whymper voyaged up the Great Bend to Fort Yukon under the Arctic Circle.

From fort to fort, from York Factory on Hudson's Bay to Fort Yukon in Alaska, the English traders transported their goods— a round trip requiring from a year to a year and a half. It was one of their deserters, in 1867, escaping down the Yukon to Bering Sea, who was the first white man to make the North-west Passage by land from the Atlantic to the Pacific. It was at this time that the first accurate description of a fair portion of the Yukon was given by Dr. W. H. Ball, of the Smithsonian Institution. But even he had never seen its source, and it was not given him to appreciate the marvel of that great natural highway.

No more remarkable river in this one particular is there in the world; taking its rise in Crater Lake, thirty miles from the ocean, the Yukon flows for twenty-five hundred miles, through the heart of the continent, ere it empties into the sea. A portage of thirty miles, and then a highway for traffic one tenth the girth of the earth!

As late as 1869, Frederick Whymper, fellow of the Royal Geographical Society, stated on hearsay that the Chilcat Indians were believed occasionally to make a short portage across the Coast Range from salt water to the head-reaches of the Yukon. But it remained for a gold hunter, questing north, ever north, to be first of all white men to cross the terrible Chilcoot Pass, and tap the Yukon at its head. This happened only the other day, but the man has become a dim legendary hero. Holt was his name, and already the mists of antiquity have wrapped about the time of his passage. 1872, 1874, and 1878 are the dates variously given—a confusion which time will never clear.

Holt penetrated as far as the Hootalinqua, and on his return to the coast reported coarse gold. The next recorded adventurer is one Edward Bean, who in 1880 headed a party of twenty-five miners from Sitka into the uncharted land. And in the same year, other parties (now forgotten, for who remembers or ever hears the wanderings of the gold hunters?) crossed the Pass, built boats out of the standing timber, and drifted down the Yukon and farther north.

And then, for a quarter of a century, the unknown and unsung heroes grappled with the frost, and groped for the gold they were sure lay somewhere among the shadows of the Pole. In the struggle with the terrifying and pitiless natural forces, they returned to the primitive, garmenting themselves in the skins of wild beasts, and covering their feet with the walrus mucluc and the moosehide moccasin. They forgot the world and its ways, as the world had forgotten them; killed their meat as they found it; feasted in plenty and starved in famine, and searched unceasingly for the yellow lure. They crisscrossed the land in every direction, threaded countless unmapped rivers in precarious birch-bark canoes, and with snowshoes and dogs broke trail through thousands of miles of silent white, where man had never been. They struggled on, under the aurora borealis or the midnight sun, through temperatures that ranged from one hundred degrees above zero to eighty degrees below, living, in the grim humour of the land, on "rabbit tracks and salmon bellies."

To-day, a man may wander away from the trail for a hundred days, and just as he is congratulating himself that at last he is treading virgin soil, he will come upon some ancient and dilapidated cabin, and forget his disappointment in wonder at the man who reared the logs. Still, if one wanders from the trail far enough and deviously enough, he may chance upon a few thousand square miles which he may have all to himself. On the other hand, no matter how far and how deviously he may wander, the possibility always remains that he may stumble, not alone upon a deserted cabin, but upon an occupied one.

As an instance of this, and of the vastness of the land, no better case need be cited than that of Harry Maxwell. An able seaman, hailing from New Bedford, Massachusetts, his ship, the brig Fannie E. Lee, was pinched in the Arctic ice. Passing from whaleship to whaleship, he eventually turned up at Point Barrow in the summer of 1880. He was NORTH of the Northland, and from this point of vantage he determined to pull south of the interior in search of gold. Across the mountains from Fort Macpherson, and a couple of hundred miles eastward from the Mackenzie, he built a cabin and established his headquarters. And here, for nineteen continuous years, he hunted his living and prospected. He ranged from the never opening ice to the north as far south as the Great Slave Lake. Here he met Warburton Pike, the author and explorer—an incident he now looks back upon as chief among the few incidents of his solitary life.

When this sailor-miner had accumulated $20,000 worth of dust he concluded that civilization was good enough for him, and proceeded "to pull for the outside." From the Mackenzie he went up the Little Peel to its headwaters, found a pass through the mountains, nearly starved to death on his way across to the Porcupine Hills, and eventually came out on the Yukon River, where he learned for the first time of the Yukon gold hunters and their discoveries. Yet for twenty years they had been working there, his next-door neighbours, virtually, in a land of such great spaces. At Victoria, British Columbia, previous to his going east over the Canadian Pacific (the existence of which he had just learned), he pregnantly remarked that he had faith in the Mackenzie watershed, and that he was going back after he had taken in the World's Fair and got a whiff or two of civilization.

Faith! It may or may not remove mountains, but it has certainly made the Northland. No Christian martyr ever possessed greater faith than did the pioneers of Alaska. They never doubted the bleak and barren land. Those who came remained, and more ever came. They could not leave. They "knew" the gold was there, and they persisted. Somehow, the romance of the land and the quest entered into their blood, the spell of it gripped hold of them and would not let them go. Man after man of them, after the most terrible privation and suffering, shook the muck of the country from his moccasins and departed for good. But the following spring always found him drifting down the Yukon on the tail of the ice jams.

Jack McQuestion aptly vindicates the grip of the North. After a residence of thirty years he insists that the climate is delightful, and declares that whenever he makes a trip to the States he is afflicted with home-sickness. Needless to say, the North still has him and will keep tight hold of him until he dies. In fact, for him to die elsewhere would be inartistic and insincere. Of three of the "pioneer" pioneers, Jack McQuestion alone survives. In 1871, from one to seven years before Holt went over Chilcoot, in the company of Al Mayo and Arthur Harper, McQuestion came into the Yukon from the North-west over the Hudson Bay Company route from the Mackenzie to Fort Yukon. The names of these three men, as their lives, are bound up in the history of the country, and so long as there be histories and charts, that long will the Mayo and McQuestion rivers and the Harper and Ladue town site of Dawson be remembered. As an agent of the Alaska Commercial Company, in 1873, McQuestion built Fort Reliance, six miles below the Klondike River. In 1898 the writer met Jack McQuestion at Minook, on the Lower Yukon. The old pioneer, though grizzled, was hale and hearty, and as optimistic as when he first journeyed into the land along the path of the Circle. And no man more beloved is there in all the North. There will be great sadness there when his soul goes questing on over the Last Divide—"farther north," perhaps—who can tell?

Frank Dinsmore is a fair sample of the men who made the Yukon country. A Yankee, born, in Auburn, Maine, the Wanderlust early laid him by the heels, and at sixteen he was heading west on the trail that led "farther north." He prospected in the Black Hills, Montana, and in the Coeur d'Alene, then heard a whisper of the North, and went up to Juneau on the Alaskan Panhandle. But the North still whispered, and more insistently, and he could not rest till he went over Chilcoot, and down into the mysterious Silent Land. This was in 1882, and he went down the chain of lakes, down the Yukon, up the Pelly, and tried his luck on the bars of McMillan River. In the fall, a perambulating skeleton, he came back over the Pass in a blizzard, with a rag of shirt, tattered overalls, and a handful of raw flour.

But he was unafraid. That winter he worked for a grubstake in Juneau, and the next spring found the heels of his moccasins turned towards salt water and his face toward Chilcoot. This was repeated the next spring, and the following spring, and the spring after that, until, in 1885, he went over the Pass for good. There was to be no return for him until he found the gold he sought.

The years came and went, but he remained true to his resolve. For eleven long years, with snow-shoe and canoe, pickaxe and gold-pan, he wrote out his life on the face of the land. Upper Yukon, Middle Yukon, Lower Yukon—he prospected faithfully and well. His bed was anywhere. Winter or summer he carried neither tent nor stove, and his six-pound sleeping-robe of Arctic hare was the warmest covering he was ever known to possess. Rabbit tracks and salmon bellies were his diet with a vengeance, for he depended largely on his rifle and fishing-tackle. His endurance equalled his courage. On a wager he lifted thirteen fifty-pound sacks of flour and walked off with them. Winding up a seven-hundred-mile trip on the ice with a forty-mile run, he came into camp at six o'clock in the evening and found a "squaw dance" under way. He should have been exhausted. Anyway, his muclucs were frozen stiff. But he kicked them off and danced all night in stocking-feet.

At the last fortune came to him. The quest was ended, and he gathered up his gold and pulled for the outside. And his own end was as fitting as that of his quest. Illness came upon him down in San Francisco, and his splendid life ebbed slowly out as he sat in his big easy-chair, in the Commercial Hotel, the "Yukoner's home." The doctors came, discussed, consulted, the while he matured more plans of Northland adventure; for the North still gripped him and would not let him go. He grew weaker day by day, but each day he said, "To-morrow I'll be all right." Other old-timers, "out on furlough,", came to see him. They wiped their eyes and swore under their breaths, then entered and talked largely and jovially about going in with him over the trail when spring came. But there in the big easy-chair it was that his Long Trail ended, and the life passed out of him still fixed on "farther north."

From the time of the first white man, famine loomed black and gloomy over the land. It was chronic with the Indians and Eskimos; it became chronic with the gold hunters. It was ever present, and so it came about that life was commonly expressed in terms of "grub"—was measured by cups of flour. Each winter, eight months long, the heroes of the frost faced starvation. It became the custom, as fall drew on, for partners to cut the cards or draw straws to determine which should hit the hazardous trail for salt water, and which should remain and endure the hazardous darkness of the Arctic night.

There was never food enough to winter the whole population. The A. C. Company worked hard to freight up the grub, but the gold hunters came faster and dared more audaciously. When the A. C. Company added a new stern-wheeler to its fleet, men said, "Now we shall have plenty." But more gold hunters poured in over the passes to the south, more voyageurs and fur traders forced a way through the Rockies from the east, more seal hunters and coast adventurers poled up from Bering Sea on the west, more sailors deserted from the whale-ships to the north, and they all starved together in right brotherly fashion. More steamers were added, but the tide of prospectors welled always in advance. Then the N. A. T. & T. Company came upon the scene, and both companies added steadily to their fleets. But it was the same old story; famine would not depart. In fact, famine grew with the population, till, in the winter of 1897-1898, the United States government was forced to equip a reindeer relief expedition. As of old, that winter partners cut the cards and drew straws, and remained or pulled for salt water as chance decided. They were wise of old time, and had learned never to figure on relief expeditions. They had heard of such things, but no mortal man of them had ever laid eyes on one.

The hard luck of other mining countries pales into insignificance before the hard luck of the North. And as for the hardship, it cannot be conveyed by printed page or word of mouth. No man may know who has not undergone. And those who have undergone, out of their knowledge, claim that in the making of the world God grew tired, and when He came to the last barrowload, "just dumped it anyhow," and that was how Alaska happened to be. While no adequate conception of the life can be given to the stay-at-home, yet the men them- selves sometimes give a clue to its rigours. One old Minook miner testified thus: "Haven't you noticed the expression on the faces of us fellows? You can tell a new-comer the minute you see him; he looks alive, enthusiastic, perhaps jolly. We old miners are always grave, unless were drinking."

Another old-timer, out of the bitterness of a "home-mood,"

imagined himself a Martian astronomer explaining to a friend, with the aid of a powerful telescope, the institutions of the earth. "There are the continents," he indicated; "and up there near the polar cap is a country, frigid and burning and lonely and apart, called Alaska. Now, in other countries and states there are great insane asylums, but, though crowded, they are insufficient; so there is Alaska given over to the worst cases. Now and then some poor insane creature comes to his senses in those awful solitudes, and, in wondering joy, escapes from the land and hastens back to his home. But most cases are incurable. They just suffer along, poor devils, forgetting their former life quite, or recalling it like a dream." Again the grip of the North, which will not let one go—for "MOST CASES ARE INCURABLE."

For a quarter of a century the battle with frost and famine went on. The very severity of the struggle with Nature seemed to make the gold hunters kindly toward one another. The latch-string was always out, and the open hand was the order of the day. Distrust was unknown, and it was no hyperbole for a man to take the last shirt off his back for a comrade. Most significant of all, perhaps, in this connection, was the custom of the old days, that when August the first came around, the prospectors who had failed to locate "pay dirt" were permitted to go upon the ground of their more fortunate comrades and take out enough for the next year's grub-stake.

In 1885 rich bar-washing was done on the Stewart River, and in 1886 Cassiar Bar was struck just below the mouth of the Hootalinqua. It was at this time that the first moderate strike was made on Forty Mile Creek, so called because it was judged to be that distance below Fort Reliance of Jack McQuestion fame. A prospector named Williams started for the outside with dogs and Indians to carry the news, but suffered such hardship on the summit of Chilcoot that he was carried dying into the store of Captain John Healy at Dyea. But he had brought the news through—COARSE GOLD! Within three months more than two hundred miners had passed in over Chilcoot, stampeding for Forty Mile. Find followed find—Sixty Mile, Miller, Glacier, Birch, Franklin, and the Koyokuk. But they were all moderate discoveries, and the miners still dreamed and searched for the fabled stream, "Too Much Gold," where gold was so plentiful that gravel had to be shovelled into the sluice-boxes in order to wash it.

And all the time the Northland was preparing to play its own huge joke. It was a great joke, albeit an exceeding bitter one, and it has led the old-timers to believe that the land is left in darkness the better part of the year because God goes away and leaves it to itself. After all the risk and toil and faithful endeavour, it was destined that few of the heroes should be in at the finish when Too Much Gold turned its yellow-treasure to the stars.

First, there was Robert Henderson—and this is true history. Henderson had faith in the Indian River district. For three years, by himself, depending mainly on his rifle, living on straight meat a large portion of the time, he prospected many of the Indian River tributaries, just missed finding the rich creeks, Sulphur and Dominion, and managed to make grub (poor grub) out of Quartz Creek and Australia Creek. Then he crossed the divide between Indian River and the Klondike, and on one of the "feeders" of the latter found eight cents to the pan. This was considered excellent in those simple days. Naming the creek "Gold Bottom," he recrossed the divide and got three men, Munson, Dalton, and Swanson, to return with him. The four took out $750. And be it emphasized, and emphasized again, THAT THIS WAS THE FIRST KLONDIKE GOLD EVER SHOVELLED IN AND WASHED OUT. And be it also emphasized, THAT ROBERT HENDERSON WAS THE DISCOVERER OF KLONDIKE, ALL LIES AND HEARSAY TALES TO THE CONTRARY.

Running out of grub, Henderson again recrossed the divide, and went down the Indian River and up the Yukon to Sixty Mile. Here Joe Ladue ran the trading post, and here Joe Ladue had originally grub-staked Henderson. Henderson told his tale, and a dozen men (all it contained) deserted the Post for the scene of his find. Also, Henderson persuaded a party of prospectors bound for Stewart River, to forgo their trip and go down and locate with him. He loaded his boat with supplies, drifted down the Yukon to the mouth of the Klondike, and towed and poled up the Klondike to Gold Bottom. But at the mouth of the Klondike he met George Carmack, and thereby hangs the tale.

Carmack was a squawman. He was familiarly known as "Siwash" George—a derogatory term which had arisen out of his affinity for the Indians. At the time Henderson encountered him he was catching salmon with his Indian wife and relatives on the site of what was to become Dawson, the Golden City of the Snows. Henderson, bubbling over with good-will, open-handed, told Carmack of his discovery. But Carmack was satisfied where he was. He was possessed by no overweening desire for the strenuous life. Salmon were good enough for him. But Henderson urged him to come on and locate, until, when he yielded, he wanted to take the whole tribe along. Henderson refused to stand for this, said that he must give the preference over Siwashes to his old Sixty Mile friends, and, it is rumoured, said some things about Siwashes that were not nice.

The next morning Henderson went on alone up the Klondike to Gold Bottom. Carmack, by this time aroused, took a short cut afoot for the same place. Accompanied by his two Indian brothers-in-law, Skookum Jim and Tagish Charley, he went up Rabbit Creek (now Bonanza), crossed into Gold Bottom, and staked near Henderson's discovery. On the way up he had panned a few shovels on Rabbit Creek, and he showed Henderson "colours" he had obtained. Henderson made him promise, if he found anything on the way back, that he would send up one of the Indians with the news. Henderson also agreed to pay for his service, for he seemed to feel that they were on the verge of something big, and he wanted to make sure.

Carmack returned down Rabbit Creek. While he was taking a

sleep on the bank about half a mile below the mouth of what was to be known as Eldorado, Skookum Jim tried his luck, and from surface prospects got from ten cents to a dollar to the pan. Carmack and his brother-in-law staked and hit "the high places" for Forty Mile, where they filed on the claims before Captain Constantine, and renamed the creek Bonanza. And Henderson was forgotten. No word of it reached him. Carmack broke his promise.

Weeks afterward, when Bonanza and Eldorado were staked from end to end and there was no more room, a party of late comers pushed over the divide and down to Gold Bottom, where they found Henderson still at work. When they told him they were from Bonanza, he was nonplussed. He had never heard of such a place. But when they described it, he recognized it as Rabbit Creek. Then they told him of its marvellous richness, and, as Tappan Adney relates, when Henderson realized what he had lost through Carmack's treachery, "he threw down his shovel and went and sat on the bank, so sick at heart that it was some time before he could speak."

Then there were the rest of the old-timers, the men of Forty Mile and Circle City. At the time of the discovery, nearly all of them were over to the west at work in the old diggings or prospecting for new ones. As they said of themselves, they were the kind of men who are always caught out with forks when it rains soup. In the stampede that followed the news of Carmack's strike very few old miners took part. They were not there to take part. But the men who did go on the stampede were mainly the worthless ones, the new-comers, and the camp hangers on. And while Bob Henderson plugged away to the east, and the heroes plugged away to the west, the greenhorns and rounders went up and staked Bonanza.

But the Northland was not yet done with its joke. When fall came on and the heroes returned to Forty Mile and to Circle City, they listened calmly to the up-river tales of Siwash discoveries and loafers' prospects, and shook their heads. They judged by the calibre of the men interested, and branded it a bunco game. But glowing reports continued to trickle down the Yukon, and a few of the old-timers went up to see. They looked over the ground—the unlikeliest place for gold in all their experience—and they went down the river again, "leaving it to the Swedes."

Again the Northland turned the tables. The Alaskan gold hunter is proverbial, not so much for his unveracity, as for his inability to tell the precise truth. In a country of exaggerations, he likewise is prone to hyperbolic description of things actual. But when it came to Klondike, he could not stretch the truth as fast as the truth itself stretched. Carmack first got a dollar pan. He lied when he said it was two dollars and a half. And when those who doubted him did get two-and-a-half pans, they said they were getting an ounce, and lo! ere the lie had fairly started on its way, they were getting, not one ounce, but five ounces. This they claimed was six ounces; but when they filled a pan of dirt to prove the lie, they washed out twelve ounces. And so it went. They continued valiantly to lie, but the truth continued to outrun them.

But the Northland's hyperborean laugh was not yet ended. When Bonanza was staked from mouth to source, those who had failed to "get in," disgruntled and sore, went up the "pups" and feeders. Eldorado was one of these feeders, and many men, after locating on it, turned their backs upon their claims and never gave them a second thought. One man sold a half-interest in five hundred feet of it for a sack of flour. Other owners wandered around trying to bunco men into buying them out for a song. And then Eldorado "showed up." It was far, far richer than Bonanza, with an average value of a thousand dollars a foot to every foot of it.

A Swede named Charley Anderson had been at work on Miller Creek the year of the strike, and arrived in Dawson with a few hundred dollars. Two miners, who had staked No. 29 Eldorado, decided that he was the proper man upon whom to "unload." He was too canny to approach sober, so at considerable expense they got him drunk. Even then it was hard work, but they kept him befuddled for several days, and finally, inveigled him into buying No. 29 for $750. When Anderson sobered up, he wept at his folly, and pleaded to have his money back. But the men who had duped him were hardhearted. They laughed at him, and kicked themselves for not having tapped him for a couple of hundred more. Nothing remained for Anderson but to work the worthless ground. This he did, and out of it he took over three-quarters of a million of dollars.

It was not till Frank Dinsmore, who already had big holdings on Birch Creek, took a hand, that the old-timers developed faith in the new diggings. Dinsmore received a letter from a man on the spot, calling it "the biggest thing in the world," and harnessed his dogs and went up to investigate. And when he sent a letter back, saying that he had never seen "anything like it," Circle City for the first time believed, and at once was precipitated one of the wildest stampedes the country had ever seen or ever will see. Every dog was taken, many went without dogs, and even the women and children and weaklings hit the three hundred miles of ice through the long Arctic night for the biggest thing in the world. It is related that but twenty people, mostly cripples and unable to travel, were left in Circle City when the smoke of the last sled disappeared up the Yukon.

Since that time gold has been discovered in all manner of places, under the grass roots of the hill-side benches, in the bottom of Monte Cristo Island, and in the sands of the sea at Nome. And now the gold hunter who knows his business shuns the "favourable looking" spots, confident in his hardwon knowledge that he will find the most gold in the least likely place. This is sometimes adduced to support the theory that the gold hunters, rather than the explorers, are the men who will ultimately win to the Pole. Who knows? It is in their blood, and they are capable of it.

PIEDMONT, CALIFORNIA., February 1902.

FOMA GORDYEEFF

"What, without asking, hither hurried WHENCE?
And, without asking, WHITHER hurried hence!
Oh, many a Cup of this forbidden Wine
Must drown the memory of that insolence!"

"Foma Gordyeeff" is a big book—not only is the breadth of Russia in it, but the expanse of life. Yet, though in each land, in this world of marts and exchanges, this age of trade and traffic, passionate figures rise up and demand of life what its fever is, in "Foma Gordyeeff" it is a Russian who so rises up and demands. For Gorky, the Bitter One, is essentially a Russian in his grasp on the facts of life and in his treatment. All the Russian self-analysis and insistent introspection are his. And, like all his brother Russians, ardent, passionate protest impregnates his work. There is a purpose to it. He writes because he has something to say which the world should hear. From that clenched fist of his, light and airy romances, pretty and sweet and beguiling, do not flow, but realities-yes, big and brutal and repulsive, but real.

He raises the cry of the miserable and the despised, and in a masterly arraignment of commercialism, protests against social conditions, against the grinding of the faces of the poor and weak, and the self-pollution of the rich and strong, in their mad lust for place and power. It is to be doubted strongly if the average bourgeois, smug and fat and prosperous, can understand this man Foma Gordyeeff. The rebellion in his blood is something to which their own does not thrill. To them it will be inexplicable that this man, with his health and his millions, could not go on living as his class lived, keeping regular hours at desk and stock exchange, driving close contracts, underbidding his competitors, and exulting in the business disasters of his fellows. It would appear so easy, and, after such a life, well appointed and eminently respectable, he could die. "Ah," Foma will interrupt rudely—he is given to rude interruptions—"if to die and disappear is the end of these money-grubbing years, why money-grub?" And the bourgeois whom he rudely interrupted will not understand. Nor did Mayakin understand as he laboured holily with his wayward godson.

"Why do you brag?" Foma, bursts out upon him. "What have you to brag about? Your son—where is he? Your daughter—what is she? Ekh, you manager of life! Come, now, you're clever, you know everything—tell me, why do you live? Why do you accumulate money? Aren't you going to die? Well, what then?" And Mayakin finds himself speechless and without answer, but unshaken and unconvinced.

Receiving by heredity the fierce, bull-like nature of his father plus the passive indomitableness and groping spirit of his mother, Foma, proud and rebellious, is repelled by the selfish, money-seeking environment into which he is born. Ignat, his father, and Mayakin, the godfather, and all the horde of successful merchants singing the paean of the strong and the praises of merciless, remorseless laissez faire, cannot entice him. Why? he demands. This is a nightmare, this life! It is without significance! What does it all mean? What is there underneath? What is the meaning of that which is underneath?

"You do well to pity people," Ignat tells Foma, the boy, "only you must use judgment with your pity. First consider the man, find out what he is like, what use can be made of him; and if you see that he is a strong and capable man, help him if you like. But if a man is weak, not inclined to work—spit upon him and go your way. And you must know that when a man complains about everything, and cries out and groans—he is not worth more than two kopeks, he is not worthy of pity, and will be of no use to you if you do help him."

Such the frank and militant commercialism, bellowed out between glasses of strong liquor. Now comes Mayakin, speaking softly and without satire:

"Eh, my boy, what is a beggar? A beggar is a man who is forced, by fate, to remind us of Christ; he is Christ's brother; he is the bell of the Lord, and rings in life for the purpose of awakening our conscience, of stirring up the satiety of man's flesh. He stands under the window and sings, 'For Christ's sa-ake!' and by that chant he reminds us of Christ, of His holy command to help our neighbour. But men have so ordered their lives that it is utterly impossible for them to act in accordance with Christ's teaching, and Jesus Christ has become entirely superfluous to us. Not once, but, in all probability, a thousand times, we have given Him over to be crucified, but still we cannot banish Him from our lives so long as His poor brethren sing His name in the streets and remind us of Him. And so now we have hit upon the idea of shutting up the beggars in such special buildings, so that they may not roam about the streets and stir up our consciences."

But Foma will have none of it. He is neither to be enticed nor cajoled. The cry of his nature is for light. He must have light. And in burning revolt he goes seeking the meaning of life. "His thoughts embraced all those petty people who toiled at hard labour. It was strange—why did they live? What satisfaction was it to them to live on the earth? All they did was to perform their dirty, arduous toil, eat poorly; they were miserably clad, addicted to drunkenness. One was sixty years old, but he still toiled side by side with young men. And they all presented themselves to Foma's imagination as a huge heap of worms, who were swarming over the earth merely to eat."

He becomes the living interrogation of life. He cannot begin living until he knows what living means, and he seeks its meaning vainly. "Why should I try to live life when I do not know what life is?" he objects when Mayakin strives with him to return and manage his business. Why should men fetch and carry for him? be slaves to him and his money?

"Work is not everything to a man," he says; "it is not true that justification lies in work . . . Some people never do any work at all, all their lives long—yet they live better than the toilers. Why is that? And what justification have I? And how will all the people who give their orders justify themselves? What have they lived for? But my idea is that everybody ought, without fail, to know solidly what he is living for. Is it possible that a man is born to toil, accumulate money, build a house, beget children, and—die? No; life means something in itself. . . . A man has been born, has lived, has died—why? All of us must consider why we are living, by God, we must! There is no sense in our life—there is no sense at all. Some are rich—they have money enough for a thousand men all to themselves— and they live without occupation; others bow their backs in toil all their life, and they haven't a penny."

But Foma can only be destructive. He is not constructive. The dim groping spirit of his mother and the curse of his environment press too heavily upon him, and he is crushed to debauchery and madness. He does not drink because liquor tastes good in his mouth. In the vile companions who purvey to his baser appetites he finds no charm. It is all utterly despicable and sordid, but thither his quest leads him and he follows the quest. He knows that everything is wrong, but he cannot right it, cannot tell why. He can only attack and demolish. "What justification have you all in the sight of God? Why do you live?" he demands of the conclave of merchants, of life's successes. "You have not constructed life—you have made a cesspool! You have disseminated filth and stifling exhalations by your deeds. Have you any conscience? Do you remember God? A five-kopek piece—that is your God! But you have expelled your conscience!"

Like the cry of Isaiah, "Go to, now, ye rich men, weep and

howl for your misfortunes that shall come upon you," is Foma's: "You blood-suckers! You live on other people's strength; you work with other people's hands! For all this you shall be made to pay! You shall perish—you shall be called to account for all! For all—to the last little tear-drop!"

Stunned by this puddle of life, unable to make sense of it, Foma questions, and questions vainly, whether of Sofya Medynsky in her drawing-room of beauty, or in the foulest depths of the first chance courtesan's heart. Linboff, whose books contradict one another, cannot help him; nor can the pilgrims on crowded steamers, nor the verse writers and harlots in dives and boozingkens. And so, wondering, pondering, perplexed, amazed, whirling through the mad whirlpool of life, dancing the dance of death, groping for the nameless, indefinite something, the magic formula, the essence, the intrinsic fact, the flash of light through the murk and dark— the rational sanction for existence, in short—Foma Gordyeeff goes down to madness and death.

It is not a pretty book, but it is a masterful interrogation of life-not of life universal, but of life particular, the social life of to-day. It is not nice; neither is the social life of to-day nice. One lays the book down sick at heart—sick for life with all its "lyings and its lusts." But it is a healthy book. So fearful is its portrayal of social disease, so ruthless its stripping of the painted charms from vice, that its tendency cannot but be strongly for good. It is a goad, to prick sleeping human cons- ciences awake and drive them into the battle for humanity.

But no story is told, nothing is finished, some one will object. Surely, when Sasha leaped overboard and swam to Foma, something happened. It was pregnant with possibilities. Yet it was not finished, was not decisive. She left him to go with the son of a rich vodka-maker. And all that was best in Sofya Medynsky was quickened when she looked upon Foma with the look of the Mother-Woman. She might have been a power for good in his life, she might have shed light into it and lifted him up to safety and honour and understanding. Yet she went away next day, and he never saw her again. No story is told, nothing is finished.

Ah, but surely the story of Foma Gordyeeff is told; his life is finished, as lives are being finished each day around us. Besides, it is the way of life, and the art of Gorky is the art of realism. But it is a less tedious realism than that of Tolstoy or Turgenev. It lives and breathes from page to page with a swing and dash and go that they rarely attain. Their mantle has fallen on his young shoulders, and he promises to wear it royally.

Even so, but so helpless, hopeless, terrible is this life of Foma Gordyeeff that we would be filled with profound sorrow for Gorky did we not know that he has come up out of the Valley of Shadow. That he hopes, we know, else would he not now be festering in a Russian prison because he is brave enough to live the hope he feels. He knows life, why and how it should be lived. And in conclusion, this one thing is manifest: Foma Gordyeeff is no mere statement of an intellectual problem. For as he lived and interrogated living, so in sweat and blood and travail has Gorky lived.

PIEDMONT, CALIFORNIA., November 1901.

THESE BONES SHALL RISE AGAIN

Rudyard Kipling, "prophet of blood and vulgarity, prince of ephemerals and idol of the unelect"—as a Chicago critic chortles—is dead. It is true. He is dead, dead and buried. And a fluttering, chirping host of men, little men and unseeing men, have heaped him over with the uncut leaves of Kim, wrapped him in Stalky & Co., for winding sheet, and for headstone reared his unconventional lines, The Lesson. It was very easy. The simplest thing in the world. And the fluttering, chirping gentlemen are rubbing their hands in amaze and wondering why they did not do it long ago, it was so very, very simple.

But the centuries to come, of which the fluttering, chirping gentlemen are prone to talk largely, will have something to say in the matter. And when they, the future centuries, quest back to the nineteenth century to find what manner of century it was—to find, not what the people of the nineteenth century thought they thought, but what they really thought, not what they thought they ought to do, but what they really did do, then a certain man, Kipling, will be read—and read with understanding. "They thought they read him with understanding, those people of the nineteenth century," the future centuries will say; "and then they thought there was no understanding in him, and after that they did not know what they thought."

But this is over-severe. It applies only to that class which serves a function somewhat similar to that served by the populace of old time in Rome. This is the unstable, mob-minded mass, which sits on the fence, ever ready to fall this side or that and indecorously clamber back again; which puts a Democratic administration into office one election, and a Republican the next; which discovers and lifts up a prophet to-day that it may stone him tomorrow; which clamours for the book everybody else is reading, for no reason under the sun save that everybody else is reading it. This is the class of whim and caprice, of fad and vogue, the unstable, incoherent, mob-mouthed, mob-minded mass, the "monkey-folk," if you please, of these latter days. Now it may be reading The Eternal City. Yesterday it was reading The Master Christian, and some several days before that it was reading Kipling. Yes, almost to his shame be it, these folk were reading him. But it was not his fault. If he depended upon them he well deserves to be dead and buried and never to rise again. But to them, let us be thankful, he never lived. They thought he lived, but he was as dead then as he is now and as he always will be.

He could not help it because he became the vogue, and it is easily understood. When he lay ill, fighting with close grapples with death, those who knew him were grieved. They were many, and in many voices, to the rim of the Seven Seas, they spoke their grief. Whereupon, and with celerity, the mob-minded mass began to inquire as to this man whom so many mourned. If everybody else mourned, it were fit that they mourn too. So a vast wail went up. Each was a spur to the other's grief, and each began privately to read this man they had never read and publicly to proclaim this man they had always read. And straightaway next day they drowned their grief in a sea of historical romance and forgot all about him. The reaction was inevitable. Emerging from the sea into which they had plunged, they became aware that they had so soon forgotten him, and would have been ashamed, had not the fluttering, chirping men said, "Come, let us bury him." And they put him in a hole, quickly, out of their sight.

And when they have crept into their own little holes, and smugly laid themselves down in their last long sleep, the future centuries will roll the stone away and he will come forth again. For be it known: THAT MAN OF US IS IMPERISHABLE WHO MAKES HIS CENTURY IMPERISHABLE. That man of us who seizes upon the salient facts of our life, who tells what we thought, what we were, and for what we stood— that man shall be the mouthpiece to the centuries, and so long as they listen he shall endure.

We remember the caveman. We remember him because he made his century imperishable. But, unhappily, we remember him dimly, in a collective sort of way, because he memorialized his century dimly, in a collective sort of way. He had no written speech, so he left us rude scratchings of beasts and things, cracked marrow-bones, and weapons of stone. It was the best expression of which he was capable. Had he scratched his own particular name with the scratchings of beasts and things, stamped his cracked marrowbones with his own particular seal, trade-marked his weapons of stone with his own particular device, that particular man would we remember. But he did the best he could, and we remember him as best we may.

Homer takes his place with Achilles and the Greek and Trojan heroes. Because he remembered them, we remember him. Whether he be one or a dozen men, or a dozen generations of men, we remember him. And so long as the name of Greece is known on the lips of men, so long will the name of Homer be known. There are many such names, linked with their times, which have come down to us, many more which will yet go down; and to them, in token that we have lived, must we add some few of our own.

Dealing only with the artist, be it understood, only those artists will go down who have spoken true of us. Their truth must be the deepest and most significant, their voices clear and strong, definite and coherent. Half-truths and partial-truths will not do, nor will thin piping voices and quavering lays. There must be the cosmic quality in what they sing. They must seize upon and press into enduring art-forms the vital facts of our existence. They must tell why we have lived, for without any reason for living, depend upon it, in the time to come, it will be as though we had never lived. Nor are the things that were true of the people a thousand years or so ago true of us to-day. The romance of Homer's Greece is the romance of Homer's Greece. That is undeniable. It is not our romance. And he who in our time sings the romance of Homer's Greece cannot expect to sing it so well as Homer did, nor will he be singing about us or our romance at all. A machine age is something quite different from an heroic age. What is true of rapid-fire guns, stock-exchanges, and electric motors, cannot possibly be true of hand-flung javelins and whirring chariot wheels. Kipling knows this. He has been telling it to us all his life, living it all his life in the work he has done.

What the Anglo-Saxon has done, he has memorialized. And by Anglo-Saxon is not meant merely the people of that tight little island on the edge of the Western Ocean. Anglo-Saxon stands for the English-speaking people of all the world, who, in forms and institutions and traditions, are more peculiarly and definitely English than anything else. This people Kipling has sung. Their sweat and blood and toil have been the motives of his songs; but underlying all the motives of his songs is the motive of motives, the sum of them all and something more, which is one with what underlies all the Anglo-Saxon sweat and blood and toil; namely, the genius of the race. And this is the cosmic quality. Both that which is true of the race for all time, and that which is true of the race for all time applied to this particular time, he has caught up and pressed into his art-forms. He has caught the dominant note of the Anglo-Saxon and pressed it into wonderful rhythms which cannot be sung out in a day and which will not be sung out in a day.

The Anglo-Saxon is a pirate, a land robber and a sea robber. Underneath his thin coating of culture, he is what he was in Morgan's time, in Drake's time, in William's time, in Alfred's time. The blood and the tradition of Hengist and Horsa are in his veins. In battle he is subject to the blood-lusts of the

Berserkers of old. Plunder and booty fascinate him immeasurably. The schoolboy of to-day dreams the dream of Clive and Hastings. The Anglo-Saxon is strong of arm and heavy of hand, and he possesses a primitive brutality all his own. There is a discontent in his blood, an unsatisfaction that will not let him rest, but sends him adventuring over the sea and among the lands in the midst of the sea. He does not know when he is beaten, wherefore the term "bulldog" is attached to him, so that all may know his unreasonableness. He has "some care as to the purity of his ways, does not wish for strange gods, nor juggle with intellectual phantasmagoria." He loves freedom, but is dictatorial to others, is self-willed, has boundless energy, and does things for himself. He is also a master of matter, an organizer of law, and an administrator of justice.

And in the nineteenth century he has lived up to his reputation. Being the nineteenth century and no other century, and in so far different from all other centuries, he has expressed himself differently. But blood will tell, and in the name of God, the Bible, and Democracy, he has gone out over the earth, possessing himself of broad lands and fat revenues, and conquering by virtue of his sheer pluck and enterprise and superior machinery.

Now the future centuries, seeking to find out what the nineteenth century Anglo-Saxon was and what were his works, will have small concern with what he did not do and what he would have liked to do. These things he did do, and for these things will he be remembered. His claim on posterity will be that in the nineteenth century he mastered matter; his twentieth-century claim will be, in the highest probability, that he organized life—but that will be sung by the twentieth-century Kiplings or the twenty-first-century Kiplings. Rudyard Kipling of the nineteenth century has sung of "things as they are." He has seen life as it is, "taken it up squarely," in both his hands, and looked upon it. What better preachment upon the Anglo-Saxon and what he has done can be had than The Bridge Builders? what better appraisement than The White

Man's Burden? As for faith and clean ideals—not of "children and gods, but men in a world of men"—who has preached them better than he?

Primarily, Kipling has stood for the doer as opposed to the dreamer—the doer, who lists not to idle songs of empty days, but who goes forth and does things, with bended back and sweated brow and work-hardened hands. The most characteristic thing about Kipling is his lover of actuality, his intense practicality, his proper and necessary respect for the hard-headed, hard-fisted fact. And, above all, he has preached the gospel of work, and as potently as Carlyle ever preached. For he has preached it not only to those in the high places, but to the common men, to the great sweating thong of common men who hear and understand yet stand agape at Carlyle's turgid utterance. Do the thing to your hand, and do it with all your might. Never mind what the thing is; so long as it is something. Do it. Do it and remember Tomlinson, sexless and soulless Tomlinson, who was denied at Heaven's gate.

The blundering centuries have perseveringly pottered and groped through the dark; but it remained for Kipling's century to roll in the sun, to formulate, in other words, the reign of law. And of the artists in Kipling's century, he of them all has driven the greater measure of law in the more consummate speech:

> Keep ye the Law—be swift in all obedience.
> Clear the land of evil, drive the road and bridge the ford.
> Make ye sure to each his own
> That he reap what he hath sown;
> By the peace among Our peoples let men know we serve the Lord.

And so it runs, from McAndrew's Law, Order, Duty, and Restraint, to his last least line, whether of The Vampire or The Recessional. And no prophet out of Israel has cried out more loudly the sins of the people, nor called them more awfully to repent.

"But he is vulgar, he stirs the puddle of life," object the fluttering, chirping gentlemen, the Tomlinsonian men. Well, and isn't life vulgar? Can you divorce the facts of life? Much of good is there, and much of ill; but who may draw aside his garment and say, "I am none of them"? Can you say that the part is greater than the whole? that the whole is more or less than the sum of the parts? As for the puddle of life, the stench is offensive to you? Well, and what then? Do you not live in it? Why do you not make it clean? Do you clamour for a filter to make clean only your own particular portion? And, made clean, are you wroth because Kipling has stirred it muddy again? At least he has stirred it healthily, with steady vigour and good-will. He has not brought to the surface merely its dregs, but its most significant values. He has told the centuries to come of our lyings and our lusts, but he has also told the centuries to come of the seriousness which is underneath our lyings and our lusts. And he has told us, too, and always has he told us, to be clean and strong and to walk upright and manlike.

"But he has no sympathy," the fluttering gentlemen chirp. "We admire his art and intellectual brilliancy, we all admire his art and intellectual brilliancy, his dazzling technique and rare rhythmical sense; but . . . he is totally devoid of sympathy." Dear! Dear! What is to be understood by this? Should he sprinkle his pages with sympathetic adjectives, so many to the paragraph, as the country compositor sprinkles commas? Surely not. The little gentlemen are not quite so infinitesimal as that. There have been many tellers of jokes, and the greater of them, it is recorded, never smiled at their own, not even in the crucial moment when the audience wavered between laughter and tears.

And so with Kipling. Take The Vampire, for instance. It has been complained that there is no touch of pity in it for the man and his ruin, no sermon on the lesson of it, no compassion for the human weakness, no indignation at the heartlessness. But are we kindergarten children that the tale be told to us in words of one syllable? Or are we men and women, able to read between the lines what Kipling intended we should read between the lines? "For some of him lived, but the most of him died." Is there not here all the excitation in the world for our sorrow, our pity, our indignation? And what more is the function of art than to excite states of consciousness complementary to the thing portrayed? The colour of tragedy is red. Must the artist also paint in the watery tears and wan-faced grief? "For some of him lived, but the most of him died"—can the heartache of the situation be conveyed more achingly? Or were it better that the young man, some of him alive but most of him dead, should come out before the curtain and deliver a homily to the weeping audience?

The nineteenth century, so far as the Anglo-Saxon is concerned, was remarkable for two great developments: the mastery of matter and the expansion of the race. Three great forces operated in it: nationalism, commercialism, democracy —the marshalling of the races, the merciless, remorseless laissez faire of the dominant bourgeoisie, and the practical, actual working government of men within a very limited equality. The democracy of the nineteenth century is not the democracy of which the eighteenth century dreamed. It is not the democracy of the Declaration, but it is what we have practised and lived that reconciles it to the fact of the "lesser breeds without the Law."

It is of these developments and forces of the nineteenth century that Kipling has sung. And the romance of it he has sung, that which underlies and transcends objective endeavour, which deals with race impulses, race deeds, and race traditions. Even into the steam-laden speech of his locomotives has he breathed our life, our spirit, our significance. As he is our mouthpiece, so are they his mouthpieces. And the romance of the nineteenth-century man as he has thus expressed himself in the nineteenth century, in shaft and wheel, in steel and steam, in far journeying and adventuring, Kipling has caught up in wondrous songs for the future centuries to sing.

If the nineteenth century is the century of the Hooligan, then is Kipling the voice of the Hooligan as surely as he is the voice of the nineteenth century. Who is more representative? Is David Harum more representative of the nineteenth century? Is Mary Johnston, Charles Major, or Winston Churchill? Is Bret Harte? William Dean Howells? Gilbert Parker? Who of them all is as essentially representative of nineteenth-century life? When Kipling is forgotten, will Robert Louis Stevenson be remembered for his Dr. Jekyll and Mr. Hyde, his Kidnapped and his David Balfour? Not so. His Treasure Island will be a classic, to go down with Robinson Crusoe, Through the Looking-Glass, and The Jungle Books. He will be remembered for his essays, for his letters, for his philosophy of life, for himself. He will be the well beloved, as he has been the well beloved. But his will be another claim upon posterity than what we are considering. For each epoch has its singer. As Scott sang the swan song of chivalry and Dickens the burgher-fear of the rising merchant class, so Kipling, as no one else, has sung the hymn of the dominant bourgeoisie, the war march of the white man round the world, the triumphant paean of commercialism and imperialism. For that will he be remembered.

OAKLAND, CALIFORNIA., October 1901.

THE OTHER ANIMALS

American journalism has its moments of fantastic hysteria, and when it is on the rampage the only thing for a rational man to do is to climb a tree and let the cataclysm go by. And so, some time ago, when the word nature-faker was coined, I, for one, climbed into my tree and stayed there. I happened to be in Hawaii at the time, and a Honolulu reporter elicited the sentiment from me that I thanked God I was not an authority on anything. This sentiment was promptly cabled to America in an Associated Press despatch, whereupon the American press (possibly annoyed because I had not climbed down out of my tree) charged me with paying for advertising by cable at a dollar per word—the very human way of the American press, which, when a man refuses to come down and be licked, makes faces at him.

But now that the storm is over, let us come and reason together. I have been guilty of writing two animal-stories—two books about dogs. The writing of these two stories, on my part, was in truth a protest against the "humanizing" of animals, of which it seemed to me several "animal writers" had been profoundly guilty. Time and again, and many times, in my narratives, I wrote, speaking of my dog-heroes: "He did not think these things; he merely did them," etc. And I did this repeatedly, to the clogging of my narrative and in violation of my artistic canons; and I did it in order to hammer into the average human understanding that these dog-heroes of mine were not directed by abstract reasoning, but by instinct, sensation, and emotion, and by simple reasoning. Also, I endeavoured to make my stories in line with the facts of evolution; I hewed them to the mark set by scientific research, and awoke, one day, to find myself bundled neck and crop into the camp of the nature-fakers.

President Roosevelt was responsible for this, and he tried to condemn me on two counts. (1) I was guilty of having a big, fighting bull-dog whip a wolf-dog. (2) I was guilty of allowing a lynx to kill a wolf-dog in a pitched battle. Regarding the second count, President Roosevelt was wrong in his field observations taken while reading my book. He must have read it hastily, for in my story I had the wolf-dog kill the lynx. Not only did I have my wolf-dog kill the lynx, but I made him eat the body of the lynx as well. Remains only the first count on which to convict me of nature-faking, and the first count does not charge me with diverging from ascertained facts. It is merely a statement of a difference of opinion. President Roosevelt does not think a bull-dog can lick a wolf-dog. I think a bull-dog can lick a wolf-dog. And there we are. Difference of opinion may make, and does make, horse-racing. I can understand that difference of opinion can make dog-fighting. But what gets me is how difference of opinion regarding the relative fighting merits of a bull-dog and a wolf-dog makes me a nature-faker and President Roosevelt a vindicated and triumphant scientist.

Then entered John Burroughs to clinch President Roosevelt's judgments. In this alliance there is no difference of opinion. That Roosevelt can do no wrong is Burroughs's opinion; and that Burroughs is always right is Roosevelt's opinion. Both are agreed that animals do not reason. They assert that all animals below man are automatons and perform actions only of two sorts—mechanical and reflex—and that in such actions no reasoning enters at all. They believe that man is the only animal capable of reasoning and that ever does reason. This is a view that makes the twentieth-century scientist smile. It is not modern at all. It is distinctly mediaeval. President Roosevelt and John Burroughs, in advancing such a view, are homo-centric in the same fashion that the scholastics of earlier and darker centuries were homocentric. Had the world not been discovered to be round until after the births of President Roosevelt and John Burroughs, they would have been geocentric as well in their theories of the Cosmos. They could not have believed otherwise. The stuff of their minds is so conditioned. They talk the argot of evolution, while they no more understand the essence and the import of evolution than does a South Sea Islander or Sir Oliver Lodge understand the noumena of radio-activity.

Now, President Roosevelt is an amateur. He may know something of statecraft and of big-game shooting; he may be able to kill a deer when he sees it and to measure it and weigh it after he has shot it; he may be able to observe carefully and accurately the actions and antics of tomtits and snipe, and, after he has observed it, definitely and coherently to convey the information of when the first chipmunk, in a certain year and a certain latitude and longitude, came out in the spring and chattered and gambolled—but that he should be able, as an individual observer, to analyze all animal life and to synthetize and develop all that is known of the method and significance of evolution, would require a vaster credulity for you or me to believe than is required for us to believe the biggest whopper ever told by an unmitigated nature-faker. No, President Roosevelt does not understand evolution, and he does not seem to have made much of an attempt to understand evolution.

Remains John Burroughs, who claims to be a thorough-going evolutionist. Now, it is rather hard for a young man to tackle an old man. It is the nature of young men to be more controlled in such matters, and it is the nature of old men, presuming upon the wisdom that is very often erroneously associated with age, to do the tackling. In this present question of nature-faking, the old men did the tackling, while I, as one young man, kept quiet a long time. But here goes at last. And first of all let Mr. Burroughs's position be stated, and stated in his words.

"Why impute reason to an animal if its behaviour can be explained on the theory of instinct?" Remember these words, for they will be referred to later. "A goodly number of persons seem to have persuaded themselves that animals do reason." "But instinct suffices for the animals . . . they get along very well without reason." "Darwin tried hard to convince himself that animals do at times reason in a rudimentary way; but Darwin was also a much greater naturalist than psychologist." The preceding quotation is tantamount, on Mr. Burroughs's part, to a flat denial that animals reason even in a rudimentary way. And when Mr. Burrough denies that animals reason even in a rudimentary way, it is equivalent to affirming, in accord with the first quotation in this paragraph, that instinct will explain every animal act that might be confounded with reason by the unskilled or careless observer.

Having bitten off this large mouthful, Mr. Burroughs proceeds with serene and beautiful satisfaction to masticate it in the following fashion. He cites a large number of instances of purely instinctive actions on the part of animals, and triumphantly demands if they are acts of reason. He tells of the robin that fought day after day its reflected image in a window-pane; of the birds in South America that were guilty of drilling clear through a mud wall, which they mistook for a solid clay bank: of the beaver that cut down a tree four times because it was held at the top by the branches of other trees; of the cow that licked the skin of her stuffed calf so affectionately that it came apart, whereupon she proceeded to eat the hay with which it was stuffed. He tells of the phobe-bird that betrays her nest on the porch by trying to hide it with moss in similar fashion to the way all phobe-birds hide their nests when they are built among rocks. He tells of the highhole that repeatedly drills through the clap-boards of an empty house in a vain attempt to find a thickness of wood deep enough in which to build its nest. He tells of the migrating lemmings of Norway that plunge into the sea and drown in vast numbers because of their instinct to swim lakes and rivers in the course of their migrations. And, having told a few more instances of like kidney, he triumphantly demands: "Where now is your much-vaunted reasoning of the lower animals?

No schoolboy in a class debate could be guilty of unfairer argument. It is equivalent to replying to the assertion that 2+2=4, by saying: "No; because 12/4=3; I have demonstrated my honourable opponent's error." When a man attacks your ability as a foot-racer, promptly prove to him that he was drunk the week before last, and the average man in the crowd of gaping listeners will believe that you have convincingly refuted the slander on your fleetness of foot. On my honour, it will work. Try it some time. It is done every day. Mr. Burroughs has done it himself, and, I doubt not, pulled the sophistical wool over a great many pairs of eyes. No, no, Mr. Burroughs; you can't disprove that animals reason by proving that they possess instincts. But the worst of it is that you have at the same time pulled the wool over your own eyes. You have set up a straw man and knocked the stuffing out of him in the complacent belief that it was the reasoning of lower animals you were knocking out of the minds of those who disagreed with you. When the highhole perforated the icehouse and let out the sawdust, you called him a lunatic . . .

But let us be charitable—and serious. What Mr. Burroughs instances as acts of instinct certainly are acts of instincts. By the same method of logic one could easily adduce a multitude of instinctive acts on the part of man and thereby prove that man is an unreasoning animal. But man performs actions of both sorts. Between man and the lower animals Mr. Burroughs finds a vast gulf. This gulf divides man from the rest of his kin by virtue of the power of reason that he alone possesses. Man is a voluntary agent. Animals are automatons. The robin fights its reflection in the window-pane because it is his instinct to fight and because he cannot reason out the physical laws that make this reflection appear real. An animal is a mechanism that operates according to fore-ordained rules. Wrapped up in its heredity, and determined long before it was born, is a certain limited capacity of ganglionic response to eternal stimuli. These responses have been fixed in the species through adaptation to environment. Natural selection has compelled the animal automatically to respond in a fixed manner and a certain way to all the usual external stimuli it encounters in the course of a usual life. Thus, under usual circumstances, it does the usual thing. Under unusual circumstances it still does the usual thing, wherefore the highhole perforating the ice-house is guilty of lunacy—of unreason, in short. To do the unusual thing under unusual circumstances, successfully to adjust to a strange environment for which his heredity has not automatically fitted an adjustment, Mr. Burroughs says is impossible. He says it is impossible because it would be a non-instinctive act, and, as is well known animals act only through instinct. And right here we catch a glimpse of Mr. Burroughs's cart standing before his horse. He has a thesis, and though the heavens fall he will fit the facts to the thesis. Agassiz, in his opposition to evolution, had a similar thesis, though neither did he fit the facts to it nor did the heavens fall. Facts are very disagreeable at times.

But let us see. Let us test Mr. Burroughs's test of reason and instinct. When I was a small boy I had a dog named Rollo. According to Mr. Burroughs, Rollo was an automaton, responding to external stimuli mechanically as directed by his instincts. Now, as is well known, the development of instinct in animals is a dreadfully slow process. There is no known case of the development of a single instinct in domestic animals in all the history of their domestication. Whatever instincts they possess they brought with them from the wild thousands of years ago. Therefore, all Rollo's actions were ganglionic discharges mechanically determined by the instincts that had been developed and fixed in the species thousands of years ago. Very well. It is clear, therefore, that in all his play with me he would act in old-fashioned ways, adjusting himself to the physical and psychical factors in his environment according to the rules of adjustment which had obtained in the wild and which had become part of his heredity.

Rollo and I did a great deal of rough romping. He chased me and I chased him. He nipped my legs, arms, and hands, often so hard that I yelled, while I rolled him and tumbled him and dragged him about, often so strenuously as to make him yelp. In the course of the play many variations arose. I would make believe to sit down and cry. All repentance and anxiety, he would wag his tail and lick my face, whereupon I would give him the laugh. He hated to be laughed at, and promptly he would spring for me with good-natured, menacing jaws, and the wild romp would go on. I had scored a point. Then he hit upon a trick. Pursuing him into the woodshed, I would find him in a far corner, pretending to sulk. Now, he dearly loved the play, and never got enough of it. But at first he fooled me. I thought I had somehow hurt his feelings and I came and knelt before him, petting him, and speaking lovingly. Promptly, in a wild outburst, he was up and away, tumbling me over on the floor as he dashed out in a mad skurry around the yard. He had scored a point.

After a time, it became largely a game of wits. I reasoned my acts, of course, while his were instinctive. One day, as he pretended to sulk in the corner, I glanced out of the woodshed doorway, simulated pleasure in face, voice, and language, and greeted one of my schoolboy friends. Immediately Rollo forgot to sulk, rushed out to see the newcomer, and saw empty space. The laugh was on him, and he knew it, and I gave it to him, too. I fooled him in this way two or three times; then be became wise. One day I worked a variation. Suddenly looking out the door, making believe that my eyes had been attracted by a moving form, I said coldly, as a child educated in turning away bill-collectors would say: "No my father is not at home." Like a shot, Rollo was out the door. He even ran down the alley to the front of the house in a vain attempt to find the man I had addressed. He came back sheepishly to endure the laugh and resume the game.

And now we come to the test. I fooled Rollo, but how was the fooling made possible? What precisely went on in that brain of his? According to Mr. Burroughs, who denies even rudimentary reasoning to the lower animals, Rollo acted instinctively, mechanically responding to the external stimulus, furnished by me, which led him to believe that a man was outside the door.

Since Rollo acted instinctively, and since all instincts are very ancient, tracing back to the pre-domestication period, we can conclude only that Rollo's wild ancestors, at the time this particular instinct was fixed into the heredity of the species, must have been in close, long-continued, and vital contact with man, the voice of man, and the expressions on the face of man. But since the instinct must have been developed during the pre-domestication period, how under the sun could his wild, undomesticated ancestors have experienced the close, long-continued, and vital contact with man?

Mr. Burroughs says that "instinct suffices for the animals," that "they get along very well without reason." But I say, what all the poor nature-fakers will say, that Rollo reasoned. He was born into the world a bundle of instincts and a pinch of brain-stuff, all wrapped around in a framework of bone, meat, and hide. As he adjusted to his environment he gained experiences. He remembered these experiences. He learned that he mustn't chase the cat, kill chickens, nor bite little girls' dresses. He learned that little boys had little boy playmates. He learned that men came into back yards. He learned that the animal man, on meeting with his own kind, was given to verbal and facial greeting. He learned that when a boy greeted a playmate he did it differently from the way he greeted a man. All these he learned and remembered. They were so many obser-vations—so many propositions, if you please. Now, what went on behind those brown eyes of his, inside that pinch of brain-stuff, when I turned suddenly to the door and greeted an imaginary person outside? Instantly, out of the thousands of observations stored in his brain, came to the front of his consciousness the particular observations connected with this particular situation. Next, he established a relation between these observations. This relation was his conclusion, achieved, as every psychologist will agree, by a definite cell-action of his grey matter. From the fact that his master turned suddenly toward the door, and from the fact that his master's voice, facial expression, and whole demeanour expressed surprise and delight, he concluded that a friend was outside. He established a relation between various things, and the act of establishing relations between things is an act of reason—of rudimentary reason, granted, but none the less of reason.

Of course Rollo was fooled. But that is no call for us to throw chests about it. How often has every last one of us been fooled in precisely similar fashion by another who turned and suddenly addressed an imaginary intruder? Here is a case in point that occurred in the West. A robber had held up a railroad train. He stood in the aisle between the seats, his revolver presented at the head of the conductor, who stood facing him. The conductor was at his mercy.

But the conductor suddenly looked over the robber's shoulder, at the same time saying aloud to an imaginary person standing at the robber's back: "Don't shoot him." Like a flash the robber whirled about to confront this new danger, and like a flash the conductor shot him down. Show me, Mr. Burroughs, where the mental process in the robber's brain was a shade different from the mental processes in Rollo's brain, and I'll quit nature-faking and join the Trappists. Surely, when a man's mental process and a dog's mental process are precisely similar, the much-vaunted gulf of Mr. Burroughs's fancy has been bridged.

I had a dog in Oakland. His name was Glen. His father was Brown, a wolf-dog that had been brought down from Alaska., and his mother was a half-wild mountain shepherd dog. Neither father nor mother had had any experience with automobiles. Glen came from the country, a half-grown puppy, to live in Oakland. Immediately he became infatuated with an automobile. He reached the culmination of happiness when he was permitted to sit up in the front seat alongside the chauffeur. He would spend a whole day at a time on an automobile debauch, even going without food. Often the machine started directly from inside the barn, dashed out the driveway without stopping, and was gone. Glen got left behind several times. The custom was established that whoever was taking the machine out should toot the horn before starting. Glen learned the signal. No matter where he was or what he was doing, when that horn tooted he was off for the barn and up into the front seat.

One morning, while Glen was on the back porch eating his breakfast of mush and milk, the chauffeur tooted. Glen rushed down the steps, into the barn, and took his front seat, the mush and milk dripping down his excited and happy chops. In passing, I may point out that in thus forsaking his breakfast for the automobile he was displaying what is called the power of choice—a peculiarly lordly attribute that, according to Mr. Burroughs, belongs to man alone. Yet Glen made his choice between food and fun.

It was not that Glen wanted his breakfast less, but that he wanted his ride more. The toot was only a joke. The automobile did not start. Glen waited and watched. Evidently he saw no signs of an immediate start, for finally he jumped out of the seat and went back to his breakfast. He ate with indecent haste, like a man anxious to catch a train. Again the horn tooted, again he deserted his breakfast, and again he sat in the seat and waited vainly for the machine to go.

They came close to spoiling Glen's breakfast for him, for he was kept on the jump between porch and barn. Then he grew wise. They tooted the horn loudly and insistently, but he stayed by his breakfast and finished it. Thus once more did he display power of choice, incidentally of control, for when that horn tooted it was all he could do to refrain from running for the barn.

The nature-faker would analyze what went on in Glen's brain somewhat in the following fashion. He had had, in his short life, experiences that not one of all his ancestors had ever had. He had learned that automobiles went fast, that once in motion it was impossible for him to get on board, that the toot of the horn was a noise that was peculiar to automobiles. These were so many propositions. Now reasoning can be defined as the act or process of the brain by which, from propositions known or assumed, new propositions are reached. Out of the propositions which I have shown were Glen's, and which had become his through the medium of his own observation of the phenomena of life, he made the new proposition that when the horn tooted it was time for him to get on board.

But on the morning I have described, the chauffeur fooled Glen. Somehow and much to his own disgust, his reasoning was erroneous. The machine did not start after all. But to reason incorrectly is very human. The great trouble in all acts of reasoning is to include all the propositions in the problem. Glen had included every proposition but one, namely, the human proposition, the joke in the brain of the chauffeur. For a number of times Glen was fooled. Then he performed another mental act. In his problem he included the human proposition (the joke in the brain of the chauffeur), and he reached the new conclusion that when the horn tooted the automobile was NOT going to start. Basing his action on this conclusion, he remained on the porch and finished his breakfast. You and I, and even Mr. Burroughs, perform acts of reasoning precisely similar to this every day in our lives. How Mr. Burroughs will explain Glen's action by the instinctive theory is beyond me. In wildest fantasy, even, my brain refuses to follow Mr. Burroughs into the primeval forest where Glen's dim ancestors, to the tooting of automobile horns, were fixing into the heredity of the breed the particular instinct that would enable Glen, a few thousand years later, capably to cope with automobiles.

Dr. C. J. Romanes tells of a female chimpanzee who was taught to count straws up to five. She held the straws in her hand, exposing the ends to the number requested. If she were asked for three, she held up three. If she were asked for four, she held up four. All this is a mere matter of training. But consider now, Mr. Burroughs, what follows. When she was asked for five straws and she had only four, she doubled one straw, exposing both its ends and thus making up the required number. She did not do this only once, and by accident. She did it whenever more straws were asked for than she possessed. Did she perform a distinctly reasoning act? or was her action the result of blind, mechanical instinct? If Mr. Burroughs cannot answer to his own satisfaction, he may call Dr. Romanes a nature-faker and dismiss the incident from his mind.

The foregoing is a trick of erroneous human reasoning that works very successfully in the United States these days. It is certainly a trick of Mr. Burroughs, of which he is guilty with distressing frequency. When a poor devil of a writer records what he has seen, and when what he has seen does not agree with Mr. Burroughs's mediaeval theory, he calls said writer a nature-faker. When a man like Mr. Hornaday comes along, Mr. Burroughs works a variation of the trick on him. Mr. Hornaday has made a close study of the orang in captivity and of the orang in its native state. Also, he has studied closely many other of the higher animal types. Also, in the tropics, he has studied the lower types of man. Mr. Hornaday is a man of experience and reputation. When he was asked if animals reasoned, out of all his knowledge on the subject he replied that to ask him such a question was equivalent to asking him if fishes swim. Now Mr. Burroughs has not had much experience in studying the lower human types and the higher animal types. Living in a rural district in the state of New York, and studying principally birds in that limited habitat, he has been in contact neither with the higher animal types nor the lower human types. But Mr. Hornaday's reply is such a facer to him and his homocentric theory that he has to do something. And he does it. He retorts: "I suspect that Mr. Hornaday is a better naturalist than he is a comparative psychologist." Exit Mr. Hornaday. Who the devil is Mr. Hornaday, anyway? The sage of Slabsides has spoken. When Darwin concluded that animals were capable of reasoning in a rudimentary way, Mr. Burroughs laid him out in the same fashion by saying: "But Darwin was also a much greater naturalist than psychologist"—and this despite Darwin's long life of laborious research that was not wholly confined to a rural district such as Mr. Burroughs inhabits in New York. Mr. Burroughs's method of argument is beautiful. It reminds one of the man whose pronunciation was vile, but who said: "Damn the dictionary; ain't I here?"

And now we come to the mental processes of Mr. Burroughs—to the psychology of the ego, if you please. Mr. Burroughs has troubles of his own with the dictionary. He violates language from the standpoint both of logic and science. Language is a tool, and definitions embodied in language should agree with the facts and history of life. But Mr. Burroughs's definitions do not so agree. This, in turn, is not the fault of his education, but of his ego. To him, despite his well-exploited and patronizing devotion to them, the lower animals are disgustingly low. To him, affinity and kinship with the other animals is a repugnant thing. He will have none of it. He is too glorious a personality not to have between him and the other animals a vast and impassable gulf. The cause of Mr. Burroughs's mediaeval view of the other animals is to be found, not in his knowledge of those other animals, but in the suggestion of his self-exalted ego. In short, Mr. Burroughs's homocentric theory has been developed out of his homocentric ego, and by the misuse of language he strives to make the facts of life agree with his theory.

After the instances I have cited of actions of animals which are impossible of explanation as due to instinct, Mr. Burroughs may reply: "Your instances are easily explained by the simple law of association." To this I reply, first, then why did you deny rudimentary reason to animals? and why did you state flatly that "instinct suffices for the animals"? And, second, with great reluctance and with overwhelming humility, because of my youth, I suggest that you do not know exactly what you do mean by that phrase "the simple law of association." Your trouble, I repeat, is with definitions. You have grasped that man performs what is called ABSTRACT reasoning, you have made a definition of abstract reason, and, betrayed by that great maker of theories, the ego, you have come to think that all reasoning is abstract and that what is not abstract reason is not reason at all. This is your attitude toward rudimentary reason. Such a process, in one of the other animals, must be either abstract or it is not a reasoning process. Your intelligence tells you that such a process is not abstract reasoning, and your homocentric thesis compels you to conclude that it can be only a mechanical, instinctive process.

Definitions must agree, not with egos, but with life. Mr. Burroughs goes on the basis that a definition is something hard and fast, absolute and eternal. He forgets that all the universe is in flux; that definitions are arbitrary and ephemeral; that they fix, for a fleeting instant of time, things that in the past were not, that in the future will be not, that out of the past become, and that out of the present pass on to the future and become other things. Definitions cannot rule life. Definitions cannot be made to rule life. Life must rule definitions or else the definitions perish.

Mr. Burroughs forgets the evolution of reason. He makes a definition of reason without regard to its history, and that definition is of reason purely abstract. Human reason, as we know it to-day, is not a creation, but a growth. Its history goes back to the primordial slime that was quick with muddy life; its history goes back to the first vitalized inorganic. And here are the steps of its ascent from the mud to man: simple reflex action, compound reflex action, memory, habit, rudimentary reason, and abstract reason. In the course of the climb, thanks to natural selection, instinct was evolved. Habit is a development in the individual. Instinct is a race-habit. Instinct is blind, unreasoning, mechanical. This was the dividing of the ways in the climb of aspiring life. The perfect culmination of instinct we find in the ant-heap and the beehive. Instinct proved a blind alley. But the other path, that of reason, led on and on even to Mr. Burroughs and you and me.

There are no impassable gulfs, unless one chooses, as Mr. Burroughs does, to ignore the lower human types and the higher animal types, and to compare human mind with bird mind. It was impossible for life to reason abstractly until speech was developed. Equipped with swords, with tools of thought, in short, the slow development of the power to reason in the abstract went on. The lowest human types do little or no reasoning in the abstract. With every word, with every increase in the complexity of thought, with every ascertained fact so gained, went on action and reaction in the grey matter of the speech discoverer, and slowly, step by step, through hundreds of thousands of years, developed the power of reason.

Place a honey-bee in a glass bottle. Turn the bottom of the bottle toward a lighted lamp so that the open mouth is away from the lamp. Vainly, ceaselessly, a thousand times, undeterred by the bafflement and the pain, the bee will hurl himself against the bottom of the bottle as he strives to win to the light. That is instinct. Place your dog in a back yard and go away. He is your dog. He loves you. He yearns toward you as the bee yearns toward the light. He listens to your departing footsteps. But the fence is too high. Then he turns his back upon the direction in which you are departing, and runs around the yard. He is frantic with affection and desire. But he is not blind. He is observant. He is looking for a hole under the fence, or through the fence, or for a place where the fence is not so high. He sees a dry-goods box standing against the fence. Presto! He leaps upon it, goes over the barrier, and tears down the street to overtake you. Is that instinct?

Here, in the household where I am writing this, is a little Tahitian "feeding-child." He believes firmly that a tiny dwarf resides in the box of my talking-machine and that it is the tiny dwarf who does the singing and the talking. Not even Mr. Burroughs will affirm that the child has reached this conclusion by an instinctive process. Of course, the child reasons the existence of the dwarf in the box. How else could the box talk and sing? In that child's limited experience it has never encountered a single instance where speech and song were produced otherwise than by direct human agency. I doubt not that the dog is considerably surprised when he hears his master's voice coming out of a box.

The adult savage, on his first introduction to a telephone, rushes around to the adjoining room to find the man who is talking through the partition. Is this act instinctive? No. Out of his limited experience, out of his limited knowledge of physics, he reasons that the only explanation possible is that a man is in the other room talking through the partition.

But that savage cannot be fooled by a hand-mirror. We must go lower down in the animal scale, to the monkey. The monkey swiftly learns that the monkey it sees is not in the glass, wherefore it reaches craftily behind the glass. Is this instinct? No. It is rudimentary reasoning. Lower than the monkey in the scale of brain is the robin, and the robin fights its reflection in the window-pane. Now climb with me for a space. From the robin to the monkey, where is the impassable gulf? and where is the impassable gulf between the monkey and the feeding-child? between the feeding-child and the savage who seeks the man behind the partition? ay, and between the savage and the astute financiers Mrs. Chadwick fooled and the thousands who were fooled by the Keeley Motor swindle?

Let us be very humble. We who are so very human are very animal. Kinship with the other animals is no more repugnant to Mr. Burroughs than was the heliocentric theory to the priests who compelled Galileo to recant. Not correct human reason, not the evidence of the ascertained fact, but pride of ego, was responsible for the repugnance.

In his stiff-necked pride, Mr. Burroughs runs a hazard more humiliating to that pride than any amount of kinship with the other animals. When a dog exhibits choice, direction, control, and reason; when it is shown that certain mental processes in that dog's brain are precisely duplicated in the brain of man; and when Mr. Burroughs convincingly proves that every action of the dog is mechanical and automatic—then, by precisely the same arguments, can it be proved that the similar actions of man are mechanical and automatic. No, Mr. Burroughs, though you stand on the top of the ladder of life, you must not kick out that ladder from under your feet. You must not deny your relatives, the other animals. Their history is your history, and if you kick them to the bottom of the abyss, to the bottom of the abyss you go yourself. By them you stand or fall. What you repudiate in them you repudiate in yourself—a pretty spectacle, truly, of an exalted animal striving to disown the stuff of life out of which it is made, striving by use of the very reason that was developed by evolution to deny the possession of evolution that developed it. This may be good egotism, but it is not good science.

PAPEETE, TAHITI., March 1908.

THE YELLOW PERIL

No more marked contrast appears in passing from our Western land to the paper houses and cherry blossoms of Japan than appears in passing from Korea to China. To achieve a correct appreciation of the Chinese the traveller should first sojourn amongst the Koreans for several months, and then, one fine day, cross over the Yalu into Manchuria. It would be of exceptional advantage to the correctness of appreciation did he cross over the Yalu on the heels of a hostile and alien army.

War is to-day the final arbiter in the affairs of men, and it is as yet the final test of the worth-whileness of peoples. Tested thus, the Korean fails. He lacks the nerve to remain when a strange army crosses his land. The few goods and chattels he may have managed to accumulate he puts on his back, along with his doors and windows, and away he heads for his mountain fastnesses. Later he may return, sans goods, chattels, doors, and windows, impelled by insatiable curiosity for a "look see." But it is curiosity merely—a timid, deerlike curiosity. He is prepared to bound away on his long legs at the first hint of danger or trouble.

Northern Korea was a desolate land when the Japanese passed through. Villages and towns were deserted. The fields lay untouched. There was no ploughing nor sowing, no green things growing. Little or nothing was to be purchased. One carried one's own food with him and food for horses and servants was the anxious problem that waited at the day's end.

In many a lonely village not an ounce nor a grain of anything could be bought, and yet there might be standing around scores of white-garmented, stalwart Koreans, smoking yard-long pipes and chattering, chattering—ceaselessly chattering. Love, money, or force could not procure from them a horseshoe or a horseshoe nail.

"Upso," was their invariable reply. "Upso," cursed word, which means "Have not got."

They had tramped probably forty miles that day, down from their hiding-places, just for a "look see," and forty miles back they would cheerfully tramp, chattering all the way over what they had seen. Shake a stick at them as they stand chattering about your camp-fire, and the gloom of the landscape will be filled with tall, flitting ghosts, bounding like deer, with great springy strides which one cannot but envy. They have splendid vigour and fine bodies, but they are accustomed to being beaten and robbed without protest or resistance by every chance foreigner who enters their country.

From this nerveless, forsaken Korean land I rode down upon the sandy islands of the Yalu. For weeks these islands had been the dread between-the-lines of two fighting armies. The air above had been rent by screaming projectiles. The echoes of the final battle had scarcely died away. The trains of Japanese wounded and Japanese dead were trailing by.

On the conical hill, a quarter of a mile away, the Russian dead were being buried in their trenches and in the shell holes made by the Japanese. And here, in the thick of it all, a man was ploughing. Green things were growing—young onions—and the man who was weeding them paused from his labour long enough to sell me a handful. Near by was the smoke-blackened ruin of the farmhouse, fired by the Russians when they retreated from the riverbed. Two men were removing the debris, cleaning the confusion, preparatory to rebuilding. They were clad in blue. Pigtails hung down their backs. I was in China!

I rode to the shore, into the village of Kuelian-Ching. There were no lounging men smoking long pipes and chattering. The previous day the Russians had been there, a bloody battle had been fought, and to-day the Japanese were there—but what was that to talk about? Everybody was busy. Men were offering eggs and chickens and fruit for sale upon the street, and bread, as I live, bread in small round loaves or buns. I rode on into the country. Everywhere a toiling population was in evidence. The houses and walls were strong and substantial. Stone and brick replaced the mud walls of the Korean dwellings. Twilight fell and deepened, and still the ploughs went up and down the fields, the sowers following after. Trains of wheelbarrows, heavily loaded, squeaked by, and Pekin carts, drawn by from four to six cows, horses, mules, ponies, or jackasses—cows even with their newborn calves tottering along on puny legs outside the traces. Everybody worked. Everything worked. I saw a man mending the road. I was in China.

I came to the city of Antung, and lodged with a merchant. He was a grain merchant. Corn he had, hundreds of bushels, stored in great bins of stout matting; peas and beans in sacks, and in the back yard his millstones went round and round, grinding out meal. Also, in his back yard, were buildings containing vats sunk into the ground, and here the tanners were at work making leather. I bought a measure of corn from mine host for my horses, and he overcharged me thirty cents. I was in China. Antung was jammed with Japanese troops. It was the thick of war. But it did not matter. The work of Antung went on just the same. The shops were wide open; the streets were lined with pedlars. One could buy anything; get anything made. I dined at a Chinese restaurant, cleansed myself at a public bath in a private tub with a small boy to assist in the scrubbing. I bought condensed milk, bitter, canned vegetables, bread, and cake. I repeat it, cake—good cake. I bought knives, forks, and spoons, granite-ware dishes and mugs. There were horseshoes and horseshoers. A worker in iron realized for me new designs of mine for my tent poles. My shoes were sent out to be repaired. A barber shampooed my hair. A servant returned with corn-beef in tins, a bottle of port, another of cognac, and beer, blessed beer, to wash out from my throat the dust of an army. It was the land of Canaan. I was in China.

The Korean is the perfect type of inefficiency—of utter worthlessness. The Chinese is the perfect type of industry. For sheer work no worker in the world can compare with him. Work is the breath of his nostrils. It is his solution of existence. It is to him what wandering and fighting in far lands and spiritual adventure have been to other peoples. Liberty to him epitomizes itself in access to the means of toil. To till the soil and labour interminably with rude implements and utensils is all he asks of life and of the powers that be. Work is what he desires above all things, and he will work at anything for anybody.

During the taking of the Taku forts he carried scaling ladders at the heads of the storming columns and planted them against the walls. He did this, not from a sense of patriotism, but for the invading foreign devils because they paid him a daily wage of fifty cents. He is not frightened by war. He accepts it as he does rain and sunshine, the changing of the seasons, and other natural phenomena. He prepares for it, endures it, and survives it, and when the tide of battle sweeps by, the thunder of the guns still reverberating in the distant canyons, he is seen calmly bending to his usual tasks. Nay, war itself bears fruits whereof he may pick. Before the dead are cold or the burial squads have arrived he is out on the field, stripping the mangled bodies, collecting the shrapnel, and ferreting in the shell holes for slivers and fragments of iron.

The Chinese is no coward. He does not carry away his doors amid windows to the mountains, but remains to guard them when alien soldiers occupy his town. He does not hide away his chickens and his eggs, nor any other commodity he possesses. He proceeds at once to offer them for sale. Nor is he to be bullied into lowering his price. What if the purchaser be a soldier and an alien made cocky by victory and confident by overwhelming force? He has two large pears saved over from last year which he will sell for five sen, or for the same price three small pears. What if one soldier persist in taking away with him three large pears? What if there be twenty other soldiers jostling about him? He turns over his sack of fruit to another Chinese and races down the street after his pears and the soldier responsible for their flight, and he does not return till he has wrenched away one large pear from that soldier's grasp.

Nor is the Chinese the type of permanence which he has been so often designated. He is not so ill-disposed toward new ideas and new methods as his history would seem to indicate. True, his forms, customs, and methods have been permanent these many centuries, but this has been due to the fact that his government was in the hands of the learned classes, and that these governing scholars found their salvation lay in suppressing all progressive ideas. The ideas behind the Boxer troubles and the outbreaks over the introduction of railroad and other foreign devil machinations have emanated from the minds of the literati, and been spread by their pamphlets and propagandists.

Originality and enterprise have been suppressed in the Chinese for scores of generations. Only has remained to him industry, and in this has he found the supreme expression of his being. On the other hand, his susceptibility to new ideas has been well demonstrated wherever he has escaped beyond the restrictions imposed upon him by his government. So far as the business man is concerned he has grasped far more clearly the Western code of business, the Western ethics of business, than has the Japanese. He has learned, as a matter of course, to keep his word or his bond. As yet, the Japanese business man has failed to understand this. When he has signed a time contract and when changing conditions cause him to lose by it, the Japanese merchant cannot understand why he should live up to his contract. It is beyond his comprehension and repulsive to his common sense that he should live up to his contract and thereby lose money. He firmly believes that the changing conditions themselves absolve him. And in so far adaptable as he has shown himself to be in other respects, he fails to grasp a radically new idea where the Chinese succeeds.

Here we have the Chinese, four hundred millions of him, occupying a vast land of immense natural resources—resources of a twentieth-century age, of a machine age; resources of coal and iron, which are the backbone of commercial civilization. He is an indefatigable worker. He is not dead to new ideas, new methods, new systems. Under a capable management he can be made to do anything. Truly would he of himself constitute the much-heralded Yellow Peril were it not for his present management. This management, his government, is set, crystallized. It is what binds him down to building as his fathers built. The governing class, entrenched by the precedent and power of centuries and by the stamp it has put upon his mind, will never free him. It would be the suicide of the governing class, and the governing class knows it.

Comes now the Japanese. On the streets of Antung, of Feng-Wang-Chang, or of any other Manchurian city, the following is a familiar scene: One is hurrying home through the dark of the unlighted streets when he comes upon a paper lantern resting on the ground. On one side squats a Chinese civilian on his hams, on the other side squats a Japanese soldier. One dips his forefinger in the dust and writes strange, monstrous characters. The other nods understanding, sweeps the dust slate level with his hand, and with his forefinger inscribes similar characters. They are talking. They cannot speak to each other, but they can write. Long ago one borrowed the other's written language, and long before that, untold generations ago, they diverged from a common root, the ancient Mongol stock.

There have been changes, differentiations brought about by diverse conditions and infusions of other blood; but down at the bottom of their being, twisted into the fibres of them, is a heritage in common—a sameness in kind which time has not obliterated. The infusion of other blood, Malay, perhaps, has made the Japanese a race of mastery and power, a fighting race through all its history, a race which has always despised commerce and exalted fighting.

To-day, equipped with the finest machines and systems of destruction the Caucasian mind has devised, handling machines and systems with remarkable and deadly accuracy, this rejuvenescent Japanese race has embarked on a course of conquest the goal of which no man knows. The head men of Japan are dreaming ambitiously, and the people are dreaming blindly, a Napoleonic dream. And to this dream the Japanese clings and will cling with bull-dog tenacity. The soldier shouting "Nippon, Banzai!" on the walls of Wiju, the widow at home in her paper house committing suicide so that her only son, her sole support, may go to the front, are both expressing the unanimity of the dream.

The late disturbance in the Far East marked the clashing of the dreams, for the Slav, too, is dreaming greatly. Granting that the Japanese can hurl back the Slav and that the two great branches of the Anglo-Saxon race do not despoil him of his spoils, the Japanese dream takes on substantiality. Japan's population is no larger because her people have continually pressed against the means of subsistence. But given poor, empty Korea for a breeding colony and Manchuria for a granary, and at once the Japanese begins to increase by leaps and bounds.

Even so, he would not of himself constitute a Brown Peril. He has not the time in which to grow and realize the dream. He is only forty-five millions, and so fast does the economic exploitation of the planet hurry on the planet's partition amongst the Western peoples that, before he could attain the stature requisite to menace, he would see the Western giants in possession of the very stuff of his dream.

The menace to the Western world lies, not in the little brown man, but in the four hundred millions of yellow men should the little brown man undertake their management. The Chinese is not dead to new ideas; he is an efficient worker; makes a good soldier, and is wealthy in the essential materials of a machine age. Under a capable management he will go far. The Japanese is prepared and fit to undertake this management. Not only has he proved himself an apt imitator of Western material progress, a sturdy worker, and a capable organizer, but he is far more fit to manage the Chinese than are we. The baffling enigma of the Chinese character is no baffling enigma to him. He understands as we could never school ourselves nor hope to understand. Their mental processes are largely the same. He thinks with the same thought-symbols as does the Chinese, and he thinks in the same peculiar grooves. He goes on where we are balked by the obstacles of incomprehension. He takes the turning which we cannot perceive, twists around the obstacle, and, presto! is out of sight in the ramifications of the Chinese mind where we cannot follow.

The Chinese has been called the type of permanence, and well he has merited it, dozing as he has through the ages. And as truly was the Japanese the type of permanence up to a generation ago, when he suddenly awoke and startled the world with a rejuvenescence the like of which the world had never seen before. The ideas of the West were the leaven which quickened the Japanese; and the ideas of the West, transmitted by the Japanese mind into ideas Japanese, may well make the leaven powerful enough to quicken the Chinese.

We have had Africa for the Afrikander, and at no distant day we shall hear "Asia for the Asiatic!" Four hundred million indefatigable workers (deft, intelligent, and unafraid to die), aroused and rejuvenescent, managed and guided by forty-five million additional human beings who are splendid fighting animals, scientific and modern, constitute that menace to the Western world which has been well named the "Yellow Peril." The possibility of race adventure has not passed away. We are in the midst of our own. The Slav is just girding himself up to begin. Why may not the yellow and the brown start out on an adventure as tremendous as our own and more strikingly unique?

The ultimate success of such an adventure the Western mind refuses to consider. It is not the nature of life to believe itself weak. There is such a thing as race egotism as well as creature egotism, and a very good thing it is. In the first place, the Western world will not permit the rise of the yellow peril. It is firmly convinced that it will not permit the yellow and the brown to wax strong and menace its peace and comfort. It advances this idea with persistency, and delivers itself of long arguments showing how and why this menace will not be permitted to arise. Today, far more voices are engaged in denying the yellow peril than in prophesying it. The Western world is warned, if not armed, against the possibility of it.

In the second place, there is a weakness inherent in the brown man which will bring his adventure to naught. From the West he has borrowed all our material achievement and passed our ethical achievement by. Our engines of production and destruction he has made his. What was once solely ours he now duplicates, rivalling our merchants in the commerce of the East, thrashing the Russian on sea and land. A marvellous imitator truly, but imitating us only in things material. Things spiritual cannot be imitated; they must be felt and lived, woven into the very fabric of life, and here the Japanese fails.

It required no revolution of his nature to learn to calculate the range and fire a field gun or to march the goose-step. It was a mere matter of training. Our material achievement is the product of our intellect. It is knowledge, and knowledge, like coin, is interchangeable. It is not wrapped up in the heredity of the new-born child, but is something to be acquired afterward. Not so with our soul stuff, which is the product of an evolution which goes back to the raw beginnings of the race. Our soul stuff is not a coin to be pocketed by the first chance comer. The Japanese cannot pocket it any more than he can thrill to short Saxon words or we can thrill to Chinese hieroglyphics. The leopard cannot change its spots, nor can the Japanese, nor can we. We are thumbed by the ages into what we are, and by no conscious inward effort can we in a day rethumb ourselves. Nor can the Japanese in a day, or a generation, rethumb himself in our image.

Back of our own great race adventure, back of our robberies by sea and land, our lusts and violences and all the evil things we have done, there is a certain integrity, a sternness of conscience, a melancholy responsibility of life, a sympathy and comradeship and warm human feel, which is ours, indubitably ours, and which we cannot teach to the Oriental as we would teach logarithms or the trajectory of projectiles. That we have groped for the way of right conduct and agonized over the soul betokens our spiritual endowment. Though we have strayed often and far from righteousness, the voices of the seers have always been raised, and we have harked back to the bidding of conscience. The colossal fact of our history is that we have made the religion of Jesus Christ our religion. No matter how dark in error and deed, ours has been a history of spiritual struggle and endeavour. We are pre-eminently a religious race, which is another way of saying that we are a right-seeking race.

"What do you think of the Japanese?" was asked an American woman after she had lived some time in Japan. "It seems to me that they have no soul," was her answer.

This must not be taken to mean that the Japanese is without soul. But it serves to illustrate the enormous difference between their souls and this woman's soul. There was no feel, no speech, no recognition. This Western soul did not dream that the Eastern soul existed, it was so different, so totally different.

Religion, as a battle for the right in our sense of right, as a yearning and a strife for spiritual good and purity, is unknown to the Japanese.

Measured by what religion means to us, the Japanese is a race without religion. Yet it has a religion, and who shall say that it is not as great a religion as ours, nor as efficacious? As one Japanese has written:

"Our reflection brought into prominence not so much the moral as the national consciousness of the individual. . . . To us the country is more than land and soil from which to mine gold or reap grain—it is the sacred abode of the gods, the spirit of our forefathers; to us the Emperor is more than the Arch Constable of a Reichsstaat, or even the Patron of a Kulturstaat; he is the bodily representative of heaven on earth, blending in his person its power and its mercy."

The religion of Japan is practically a worship of the State itself. Patriotism is the expression of this worship. The Japanese mind does not split hairs as to whether the Emperor is Heaven incarnate or the State incarnate. So far as the Japanese are concerned, the Emperor lives, is himself deity. The Emperor is the object to live for and to die for. The Japanese is not an individualist. He has developed national consciousness instead of moral consciousness. He is not interested in his own moral welfare except in so far as it is the welfare of the State. The honour of the individual, per se, does not exist. Only exists the honour of the State, which is his honour. He does not look upon himself as a free agent, working out his own personal salvation. Spiritual agonizing is unknown to him. He has a "sense of calm trust in fate, a quiet submission to the inevitable, a stoic composure in sight of danger or calamity, a disdain of life and friendliness with death." He relates himself to the State as, amongst bees, the worker is related to the hive; himself nothing, the State everything; his reasons for existence the exaltation and glorification of the State.

The most admired quality to-day of the Japanese is his patriotism. The Western world is in rhapsodies over it, unwittingly measuring the Japanese patriotism by its own conceptions of patriotism. "For God, my country, and the Czar!" cries the Russian patriot; but in the Japanese mind there is no differentiation between the three. The Emperor is the Emperor, and God and country as well. The patriotism of the Japanese is blind and unswerving loyalty to what is practically an absolutism. The Emperor can do no wrong, nor can the five ambitious great men who have his ear and control the destiny of Japan.

No great race adventure can go far nor endure long which has no deeper foundation than material success, no higher prompting than conquest for conquest's sake and mere race glorification. To go far and to endure, it must have behind it an ethical impulse, a sincerely conceived righteousness. But it must be taken into consideration that the above postulate is itself a product of Western race-egotism, urged by our belief in our own righteousness and fostered by a faith in ourselves which may be as erroneous as are most fond race fancies. So be it. The world is whirling faster to-day than ever before. It has gained impetus. Affairs rush to conclusion. The Far East is the point of contact of the adventuring Western people as well as of the Asiatic. We shall not have to wait for our children's time nor our children's children. We shall ourselves see and largely determine the adventure of the Yellow and the Brown.

FENG-WANG-CHENG, MANCHURIA., June 1904,

WHAT LIFE MEANS TO ME

I was born in the working-class. Early I discovered enthusiasm, ambition, and ideals; and to satisfy these became the problem of my child-life. My environment was crude and rough and raw. I had no outlook, but an uplook rather. My place in society was at the bottom. Here life offered nothing but sordidness and wretchedness, both of the flesh and the spirit; for here flesh and spirit were alike starved and tormented.

Above me towered the colossal edifice of society, and to my mind the only way out was up. Into this edifice I early resolved to climb. Up above, men wore black clothes and boiled shirts, and women dressed in beautiful gowns. Also, there were good things to eat, and there was plenty to eat. This much for the flesh. Then there were the things of the spirit. Up above me, I knew, were unselfishnesses of the spirit, clean and noble thinking, keen intellectual living. I knew all this because I read "Seaside Library" novels, in which, with the exception of the villains and adventuresses, all men and women thought beautiful thoughts, spoke a beautiful tongue, and performed glorious deeds. In short, as I accepted the rising of the sun, I accepted that up above me was all that was fine and noble and gracious, all that gave decency and dignity to life, all that made life worth living and that remunerated one for his travail and misery.

But it is not particularly easy for one to climb up out of the working-class—especially if he is handicapped by the possession of ideals and illusions. I lived on a ranch in

California, and was hard put to find the ladder whereby to climb. I early inquired the rate of interest on invested money, and worried my child's brain into an understanding of the virtues and excellences of that remarkable invention of man, compound interest. Further, I ascertained the current rates of wages for workers of all ages, and the cost of living. From all this data I concluded that if I began immediately and worked and saved until I was fifty years of age, I could then stop working and enter into participation in a fair portion of the delights and goodnesses that would then be open to me higher up in society. Of course, I resolutely determined not to marry, while I quite forgot to consider at all that great rock of disaster in the working-class world—sickness.

But the life that was in me demanded more than a meagre existence of scraping and scrimping. Also, at ten years of age, I became a newsboy on the streets of a city, and found myself with a changed uplook. All about me were still the same sordidness and wretchedness, and up above me was still the same paradise waiting to be gained; but the ladder whereby to climb was a different one. It was now the ladder of business. Why save my earnings and invest in government bonds, when, by buying two newspapers for five cents, with a turn of the wrist I could sell them for ten cents and double my capital? The business ladder was the ladder for me, and I had a vision of myself becoming a bald-headed and successful merchant prince.

Alas for visions! When I was sixteen I had already earned the title of "prince." But this title was given me by a gang of cut-throats and thieves, by whom I was called "The Prince of the Oyster Pirates." And at that time I had climbed the first rung of the business ladder. I was a capitalist. I owned a boat and a complete oyster-pirating outfit. I had begun to exploit my fellow-creatures. I had a crew of one man. As captain and owner I took two-thirds of the spoils, and gave the crew one-third, though the crew worked just as hard as I did and risked just as much his life and liberty.

This one rung was the height I climbed up the business ladder. One night I went on a raid amongst the Chinese fishermen. Ropes and nets were worth dollars and cents. It was robbery, I grant, but it was precisely the spirit of capitalism. The capitalist takes away the possessions of his fellow-creatures by means of a rebate, or of a betrayal of trust, or by the purchase of senators and supreme-court judges. I was merely crude. That was the only difference. I used a gun.

But my crew that night was one of those inefficients against whom the capitalist is wont to fulminate, because, forsooth, such inefficients increase expenses and reduce dividends. My crew did both. What of his carelessness he set fire to the big mainsail and totally destroyed it. There weren't any dividends that night, and the Chinese fishermen were richer by the nets and ropes we did not get. I was bankrupt, unable just then to pay sixty-five dollars for a new mainsail. I left my boat at anchor and went off on a bay-pirate boat on a raid up the Sacramento River. While away on this trip, another gang of bay pirates raided my boat. They stole everything, even the anchors; and later on, when I recovered the drifting hulk, I sold it for twenty dollars. I had slipped back the one rung I had climbed, and never again did I attempt the business ladder.

From then on I was mercilessly exploited by other capitalists. I had the muscle, and they made money out of it while I made but a very indifferent living out of it. I was a sailor before the mast, a longshoreman, a roustabout; I worked in canneries, and factories, and laundries; I mowed lawns, and cleaned carpets, and washed windows. And I never got the full product of my toil. I looked at the daughter of the cannery owner, in her carriage, and knew that it was my muscle, in part, that helped drag along that carriage on its rubber tyres. I looked at the son of the factory owner, going to college, and knew that it was my muscle that helped, in part, to pay for the wine and good fellowship he enjoyed.

But I did not resent this. It was all in the game. They were the strong. Very well, I was strong. I would carve my way to a place amongst them and make money out of the muscles of other men. I was not afraid of work. I loved hard work. I would pitch in and work harder than ever and eventually become a pillar of society.

And just then, as luck would have it, I found an employer that was of the same mind. I was willing to work, and he was more than willing that I should work. I thought I was learning a trade. In reality, I had displaced two men. I thought he was making an electrician out of me; as a matter of fact, he was making fifty dollars per month out of me. The two men I had displaced had received forty dollars each per month; I was doing the work of both for thirty dollars per month.

This employer worked me nearly to death. A man may love oysters, but too many oysters will disincline him toward that particular diet. And so with me. Too much work sickened me. I did not wish ever to see work again. I fled from work. I became a tramp, begging my way from door to door, wandering over the United States and sweating bloody sweats in slums and prisons.

I had been born in the working-class, and I was now, at the age of eighteen, beneath the point at which I had started. I was down in the cellar of society, down in the subterranean depths of misery about which it is neither nice nor proper to speak. I was in the pit, the abyss, the human cesspool, the shambles and the charnel-house of our civilization. This is the part of the edifice of society that society chooses to ignore. Lack of space compels me here to ignore it, and I shall say only that the things I there saw gave me a terrible scare.

I was scared into thinking. I saw the naked simplicities of the complicated civilization in which I lived. Life was a matter of food and shelter. In order to get food and shelter men sold things. The merchant sold shoes, the politician sold his manhood, and the representative of the people, with exceptions, of course, sold his trust; while nearly all sold their honour. Women, too, whether on the street or in the holy bond of wedlock, were prone to sell their flesh. All things were commodities, all people bought and sold. The one commodity that labour had to sell was muscle. The honour of labour had no price in the marketplace. Labour had muscle, and muscle alone, to sell.

But there was a difference, a vital difference. Shoes and trust and honour had a way of renewing themselves. They were imperishable stocks. Muscle, on the other hand, did not renew. As the shoe merchant sold shoes, he continued to replenish his stock. But there was no way of replenishing the labourer's stock of muscle. The more he sold of his muscle, the less of it remained to him. It was his one commodity, and each day his stock of it diminished. In the end, if he did not die before, he sold out and put up his shutters. He was a muscle bankrupt, and nothing remained to him but to go down into the cellar of society and perish miserably.

I learned, further, that brain was likewise a commodity. It, too, was different from muscle. A brain seller was only at his prime when he was fifty or sixty years old, and his wares were fetching higher prices than ever. But a labourer was worked out or broken down at forty-five or fifty. I had been in the cellar of society, and I did not like the place as a habitation. The pipes and drains were unsanitary, and the air was bad to breathe. If I could not live on the parlour floor of society, I could, at any rate, have a try at the attic. It was true, the diet there was slim, but the air at least was pure. So I resolved to sell no more muscle, and to become a vendor of brains.

Then began a frantic pursuit of knowledge. I returned to California and opened the books. While thus equipping myself to become a brain merchant, it was inevitable that I should delve into sociology. There I found, in a certain class of books, scientifically formulated, the simple sociological concepts I had already worked out for myself. Other and greater minds, before I was born, had worked out all that I had thought and a vast deal more. I discovered that I was a socialist.

The socialists were revolutionists, inasmuch as they struggled to overthrow the society of the present, and out of the material to build the society of the future. I, too, was a socialist and a revolutionist. I joined the groups of working-class and intellectual revolutionists, and for the first time came into intellectual living. Here I found keen-flashing intellects and brilliant wits; for here I met strong and alert-brained, withal horny-handed, members of the working-class; unfrocked preachers too wide in their Christianity for any congregation of Mammon-worshippers; professors broken on the wheel of university subservience to the ruling class and flung out because they were quick with knowledge which they strove to apply to the affairs of mankind.

Here I found, also, warm faith in the human, glowing idealism, sweetnesses of unselfishness, renunciation, and martyrdom—all the splendid, stinging things of the spirit. Here life was clean, noble, and alive. Here life rehabilitated itself, became wonderful and glorious; and I was glad to be alive. I was in touch with great souls who exalted flesh and spirit over dollars and cents, and to whom the thin wail of the starved slum child meant more than all the pomp and circumstance of commercial expansion and world empire. All about me were nobleness of purpose and heroism of effort, and my days and nights were sunshine and starshine, all fire and dew, with before my eyes, ever burning and blazing, the Holy Grail, Christ's own Grail, the warm human, long-suffering and maltreated, but to be rescued and saved at the last.

And I, poor foolish I, deemed all this to be a mere foretaste of the delights of living I should find higher above me in society. I had lost many illusions since the day I read "Seaside Library" novels on the California ranch. I was destined to lose many of the illusions I still retained.

As a brain merchant I was a success. Society opened its portals to me. I entered right in on the parlour floor, and my disillusionment proceeded rapidly. I sat down to dinner with the masters of society, and with the wives and daughters of the masters of society. The women were gowned beautifully, I admit; but to my naive surprise I discovered that they were of the same clay as all the rest of the women I had known down below in the cellar. "The colonel's lady and Judy O'Grady were sisters under their skins"—and gowns.

It was not this, however, so much as their materialism, that shocked me. It is true, these beautifully gowned, beautiful women prattled sweet little ideals and dear little moralities; but in spite of their prattle the dominant key of the life they lived was materialistic. And they were so sentimentally selfish! They assisted in all kinds of sweet little charities, and informed one of the fact, while all the time the food they ate and the beautiful clothes they wore were bought out of dividends stained with the blood of child labour, and sweated labour, and of prostitution itself. When I mentioned such facts, expecting in my innocence that these sisters of Judy O'Grady would at once strip off their blood-dyed silks and jewels, they became excited and angry, and read me preachments about the lack of thrift, the drink, and the innate depravity that caused all the misery in society's cellar. When I mentioned that I couldn't quite see that it was the lack of thrift, the intemperance, and the depravity of a half-starved child of six that made it work twelve hours every night in a Southern cotton mill, these sisters of Judy O'Grady attacked my private life and called me an "agitator"—as though that, forsooth, settled the argument.

Nor did I fare better with the masters themselves. I had expected to find men who were clean, noble, and alive, whose ideals were clean, noble, and alive. I went about amongst the men who sat in the high places—the preachers, the politicians, the business men, the professors, and the editors. I ate meat with them, drank wine with them, automobiled with them, and studied them. It is true, I found many that were clean and noble; but with rare exceptions, they were not ALIVE. I do verily believe I could count the exceptions on the fingers of my two hands. Where they were not alive with rottenness, quick with unclean life, there were merely the unburied dead—clean and noble, like well-preserved mummies, but not alive. In this connection I may especially mention the professors I met, the men who live up to that decadent university ideal, "the passionless pursuit of passionless intelligence."

I met men who invoked the name of the Prince of Peace in their diatribes against war, and who put rifles in the hands of Pinkertons with which to shoot down strikers in their own factories. I met men incoherent with indignation at the brutality of prize-fighting, and who, at the same time, were parties to the adulteration of food that killed each year more babies than even red-handed Herod had killed.

I talked in hotels and clubs and homes and Pullmans, and steamer-chairs with captains of industry, and marvelled at how little travelled they were in the realm of intellect. On the other hand, I discovered that their intellect, in the business sense, was abnormally developed. Also, I discovered that their morality, where business was concerned, was nil.

This delicate, aristocratic-featured gentleman, was a dummy director and a tool of corporations that secretly robbed widows and orphans. This gentleman, who collected fine editions and was an especial patron of literature, paid blackmail to a heavy-jowled, black-browed boss of a municipal machine. This editor, who published patent medicine advertisements and did not dare print the truth in his paper about said patent medicines for fear of losing the advertising, called me a scoundrelly demagogue because I told him that his political economy was antiquated and that his biology was contemporaneous with Pliny.

This senator was the tool and the slave, the little puppet of a gross, uneducated machine boss; so was this governor and this supreme court judge; and all three rode on railroad passes. This man, talking soberly and earnestly about the beauties of idealism and the goodness of God, had just betrayed his comrades in a business deal. This man, a pillar of the church and heavy contributor to foreign missions, worked his shop girls ten hours a day on a starvation wage and thereby directly encouraged prostitution. This man, who endowed chairs in universities, perjured himself in courts of law over a matter of dollars and cents. And this railroad magnate broke his word as a gentleman and a Christian when he granted a secret rebate to one of two captains of industry locked together in a struggle to the death.

It was the same everywhere, crime and betrayal, betrayal and crime—men who were alive, but who were neither clean nor noble, men who were clean and noble, but who were not alive. Then there was a great, hopeless mass, neither noble nor alive, but merely clean. It did not sin positively nor deliberately; but it did sin passively and ignorantly by acquiescing in the current immorality and profiting by it. Had it been noble and alive it would not have been ignorant, and it would have refused to share in the profits of betrayal and crime.

I discovered that I did not like to live on the parlour floor of society. Intellectually I was as bored. Morally and spiritually I was sickened. I remembered my intellectuals and idealists, my unfrocked preachers, broken professors, and clean-minded, class-conscious working-men. I remembered my days and nights of sunshine and starshine, where life was all a wild sweet wonder, a spiritual paradise of unselfish adventure and ethical romance. And I saw before me, ever blazing and burning, the Holy Grail.

So I went back to the working-class, in which I had been born and where I belonged. I care no longer to climb. The imposing edifice of society above my head holds no delights for me. It is the foundation of the edifice that interests me. There I am content to labour, crowbar in hand, shoulder to shoulder with intellectuals, idealists, and class-conscious working-men, getting a solid pry now and again and setting the whole edifice rocking. Some day, when we get a few more hands and crowbars to work, we'll topple it over, along with all its rotten life and unburied dead, its monstrous selfishness and sodden materialism. Then we'll cleanse the cellar and build a new habitation for mankind, in which there will be no parlour floor, in which all the rooms will be bright and airy, and where the air that is breathed will be clean, noble, and alive.

Such is my outlook. I look forward to a time when man shall progress upon something worthier and higher than his stomach, when there will be a finer incentive to impel men to action than the incentive of to-day, which is the incentive of the stomach. I retain my belief in the nobility and excellence of the human. I believe that spiritual sweetness and unselfishness will conquer the gross gluttony of to-day. And last of all, my faith is in the working-class. As some Frenchman has said, "The stairway of time is ever echoing with the wooden shoe going up, the polished boot descending."

NEWTON, IOWA., November 1905.

ABOUT THE AUTHOR

 **Jack London,** probably born John Griffith Chaney (January 12, 1876 – November 22, 1916) was an American author who wrote The Call of the Wild and over fifty other books. A pioneer in the then-burgeoning world of commercial magazine fiction, he was one of the first Americans to make a huge financial success from writing.

Clarice Stasz and other biographers believe it to be likely that Jack London's biological father was astrologer William Chaney. Chaney was a professor of astrology; according to Stasz, "From the viewpoint of serious astrologers today, Chaney is a major figure who shifted the practice from quackery to a more rigorous method."

A pivotal event was his discovery in 1886 of the Oakland Public Library and a sympathetic librarian, Ina Coolbrith (who later became California's first poet laureate and an important figure in the San Francisco literary community).

In later life Jack London indulged his very wide-ranging interests with a personal library of 15,000 volumes, referring to his books as "the tools of my trade."

Choose from Thousands of 1stWorldLibrary Classics By

A. M. Barnard	Booth Tarkington	Edward Everett Hale
Ada Leverson	Boyd Cable	Edward J. O'Biren
Adolphus William Ward	Bram Stoker	Edward S. Ellis
Aesop	C. Collodi	Edwin L. Arnold
Agatha Christie	C. E. Orr	Eleanor Atkins
Alexander Aaronsohn	C. M. Ingleby	Eleanor Hallowell Abbott
Alexander Kielland	Carolyn Wells	Eliot Gregory
Alexandre Dumas	Catherine Parr Traill	Elizabeth Gaskell
Alfred Gatty	Charles A. Eastman	Elizabeth McCracken
Alfred Ollivant	Charles Amory Beach	Elizabeth Von Arnim
Alice Duer Miller	Charles Dickens	Ellem Key
Alice Turner Curtis	Charles Dudley Warner	Emerson Hough
Alice Dunbar	Charles Farrar Browne	Emilie F. Carlen
Allen Chapman	Charles Ives	Emily Bronte
Alleyne Ireland	Charles Kingsley	Emily Dickinson
Ambrose Bierce	Charles Klein	Enid Bagnold
Amelia E. Barr	Charles Hanson Towne	Enilor Macartney Lane
Amory H. Bradford	Charles Lathrop Pack	Erasmus W. Jones
Andrew Lang	Charles Romyn Dake	Ernie Howard Pie
Andrew McFarland Davis	Charles Whibley	Ethel May Dell
Andy Adams	Charles Willing Beale	Ethel Turner
Angela Brazil	Charlotte M. Braeme	Ethel Watts Mumford
Anna Alice Chapin	Charlotte M. Yonge	Eugene Sue
Anna Sewell	Charlotte Perkins Stetson	Eugenie Foa
Annie Besant	Clair W. Hayes	Eugene Wood
Annie Hamilton Donnell	Clarence Day Jr.	Eustace Hale Ball
Annie Payson Call	Clarence E. Mulford	Evelyn Everett-green
Annie Roe Carr	Clemence Housman	Everard Cotes
Annonaymous	Confucius	F. H. Cheley
Anton Chekhov	Coningsby Dawson	F. J. Cross
Archibald Lee Fletcher	Cornelis DeWitt Wilcox	F. Marion Crawford
Arnold Bennett	Cyril Burleigh	Fannie E. Newberry
Arthur C. Benson	D. H. Lawrence	Federick Austin Ogg
Arthur Conan Doyle	Daniel Defoe	Ferdinand Ossendowski
Arthur M. Winfield	David Garnett	Fergus Hume
Arthur Ransome	Dinah Craik	Florence A. Kilpatrick
Arthur Schnitzler	Don Carlos Janes	Fremont B. Deering
Arthur Train	Donald Keyhoe	Francis Bacon
Atticus	Dorothy Kilner	Francis Darwin
B.H. Baden-Powell	Dougan Clark	Frances Hodgson Burnett
B. M. Bower	Douglas Fairbanks	Frances Parkinson Keyes
B. C. Chatterjee	E. Nesbit	Frank Gee Patchin
Baroness Emmuska Orczy	E. P. Roe	Frank Harris
Baroness Orczy	E. Phillips Oppenheim	Frank Jewett Mather
Basil King	E. S. Brooks	Frank L. Packard
Bayard Taylor	Earl Barnes	Frank V. Webster
Ben Macomber	Edgar Rice Burroughs	Frederic Stewart Isham
Bertha Muzzy Bower	Edith Van Dyne	Frederick Trevor Hill
Bjornstjerne Bjornson	Edith Wharton	Frederick Winslow Taylor

Friedrich Kerst	Hayden Carruth	James Branch Cabell
Friedrich Nietzsche	Helent Hunt Jackson	James DeMille
Fyodor Dostoyevsky	Helen Nicolay	James Joyce
G.A. Henty	Hendrik Conscience	James Lane Allen
G.K. Chesterton	Hendy David Thoreau	James Lane Allen
Gabrielle E. Jackson	Henri Barbusse	James Oliver Curwood
Garrett P. Serviss	Henrik Ibsen	James Oppenheim
Gaston Leroux	Henry Adams	James Otis
George A. Warren	Henry Ford	James R. Driscoll
George Ade	Henry Frost	Jane Abbott
Geroge Bernard Shaw	Henry James	Jane Austen
George Cary Eggleston	Henry Jones Ford	Jane L. Stewart
George Durston	Henry Seton Merriman	Janet Aldridge
George Ebers	Henry W Longfellow	Jens Peter Jacobsen
George Eliot	Herbert A. Giles	Jerome K. Jerome
George Gissing	Herbert Carter	Jessie Graham Flower
George MacDonald	Herbert N. Casson	John Buchan
George Meredith	Herman Hesse	John Burroughs
George Orwell	Hildegard G. Frey	John Cournos
George Sylvester Viereck	Homer	John F. Kennedy
George Tucker	Honore De Balzac	John Gay
George W. Cable	Horace B. Day	John Glasworthy
George Wharton James	Horace Walpole	John Habberton
Gertrude Atherton	Horatio Alger Jr.	John Joy Bell
Gordon Casserly	Howard Pyle	John Kendrick Bangs
Grace E. King	Howard R. Garis	John Milton
Grace Gallatin	Hugh Lofting	John Philip Sousa
Grace Greenwood	Hugh Walpole	John Taintor Foote
Grant Allen	Humphry Ward	Jonas Lauritz Idemil Lie
Guillermo A. Sherwell	Ian Maclaren	Jonathan Swift
Gulielma Zollinger	Inez Haynes Gillmore	Joseph A. Altsheler
Gustav Flaubert	Irving Bacheller	Joseph Carey
H. A. Cody	Isabel Cecilia Williams	Joseph Conrad
H. B. Irving	Isabel Hornibrook	Joseph E. Badger Jr
H.C. Bailey	Israel Abrahams	Joseph Hergesheimer
H. G. Wells	Ivan Turgenev	Joseph Jacobs
H. H. Munro	J.G.Austin	Jules Vernes
H. Irving Hancock	J. Henri Fabre	Julian Hawthrone
H. R. Naylor	J. M. Barrie	Julie A Lippmann
H. Rider Haggard	J. M. Walsh	Justin Huntly McCarthy
H. W. C. Davis	J. Macdonald Oxley	Kakuzo Okakura
Haldeman Julius	J. R. Miller	Karle Wilson Baker
Hall Caine	J. S. Fletcher	Kate Chopin
Hamilton Wright Mabie	J. S. Knowles	Kenneth Grahame
Hans Christian Andersen	J. Storer Clouston	Kenneth McGaffey
Harold Avery	J. W. Duffield	Kate Langley Bosher
Harold McGrath	Jack London	Kate Langley Bosher
Harriet Beecher Stowe	Jacob Abbott	Katherine Cecil Thurston
Harry Castlemon	James Allen	Katherine Stokes
Harry Coghill	James Andrews	L. A. Abbot
Harry Houidini	James Baldwin	L. T. Meade

L. Frank Baum
Latta Griswold
Laura Dent Crane
Laura Lee Hope
Laurence Housman
Lawrence Beasley
Leo Tolstoy
Leonid Andreyev
Lewis Carroll
Lewis Sperry Chafer
Lilian Bell
Lloyd Osbourne
Louis Hughes
Louis Joseph Vance
Louis Tracy
Louisa May Alcott
Lucy Fitch Perkins
Lucy Maud Montgomery
Luther Benson
Lydia Miller Middleton
Lyndon Orr
M. Corvus
M. H. Adams
Margaret E. Sangster
Margret Howth
Margaret Vandercook
Margaret W. Hungerford
Margret Penrose
Maria Edgeworth
Maria Thompson Daviess
Mariano Azuela
Marion Polk Angellotti
Mark Overton
Mark Twain
Mary Austin
Mary Catherine Crowley
Mary Cole
Mary Hastings Bradley
Mary Roberts Rinehart
Mary Rowlandson
M. Wollstonecraft Shelley
Maud Lindsay
Max Beerbohm
Myra Kelly
Nathaniel Hawthrone
Nicolo Machiavelli
O. F. Walton
Oscar Wilde

Owen Johnson
P.G. Wodehouse
Paul and Mabel Thorne
Paul G. Tomlinson
Paul Severing
Percy Brebner
Percy Keese Fitzhugh
Peter B. Kyne
Plato
Quincy Allen
R. Derby Holmes
R. L. Stevenson
R. S. Ball
Rabindranath Tagore
Rahul Alvares
Ralph Bonehill
Ralph Henry Barbour
Ralph Victor
Ralph Waldo Emmerson
Rene Descartes
Ray Cummings
Rex Beach
Rex E. Beach
Richard Harding Davis
Richard Jefferies
Richard Le Gallienne
Robert Barr
Robert Frost
Robert Gordon Anderson
Robert L. Drake
Robert Lansing
Robert Lynd
Robert Michael Ballantyne
Robert W. Chambers
Rosa Nouchette Carey
Rudyard Kipling
Saint Augustine
Samuel B. Allison
Samuel Hopkins Adams
Sarah Bernhardt
Sarah C. Hallowell
Selma Lagerlof
Sherwood Anderson
Sigmund Freud
Standish O'Grady
Stanley Weyman
Stella Benson
Stella M. Francis

Stephen Crane
Stewart Edward White
Stijn Streuvels
Swami Abhedananda
Swami Parmananda
T. S. Ackland
T. S. Arthur
The Princess Der Ling
Thomas A. Janvier
Thomas A Kempis
Thomas Anderton
Thomas Bailey Aldrich
Thomas Bulfinch
Thomas De Quincey
Thomas Dixon
Thomas H. Huxley
Thomas Hardy
Thomas More
Thornton W. Burgess
U. S. Grant
Upton Sinclair
Valentine Williams
Various Authors
Vaughan Kester
Victor Appleton
Victor G. Durham
Victoria Cross
Virginia Woolf
Wadsworth Camp
Walter Camp
Walter Scott
Washington Irving
Wilbur Lawton
Wilkie Collins
Willa Cather
Willard F. Baker
William Dean Howells
William le Queux
W. Makepeace Thackeray
William W. Walter
William Shakespeare
Winston Churchill
Yei Theodora Ozaki
Yogi Ramacharaka
Young E. Allison
Zane Grey